RANDY
ALCORN

Seeing the
UNSEEN

a daily dose of eternal perspective

epm eternal perspective ministries
with Randy Alcorn

Cover Design: Stephanie Anderson
Cover Photo © Dave Morrow, www.davemorrowphotography.com

Seeing the Unseen: A Daily Dose of Eternal Perspective
© 2013 by Randy Alcorn
Published by Eternal Perspective Ministries
Sandy, Oregon 97055

ISBN-10: 0-9700016-6-5
ISBN-13: 978-0-9700016-6-5

Printed in the United States of America

We hope you enjoy this book from Eternal Perspective Ministries. For more information on other books and products available from EPM, go to www.epm.org.

15 16 17 18 – 6 5 4 3

*Many thanks to Stephanie Anderson
who helped compile and assemble my
writings in this book, and Doreen Button
who assisted in the editing.*

FIXING OUR EYES ON THE UNSEEN

Do you have a life verse? Mine's 2 Corinthians 4:18. It's on our web page and at the end of every email I send:

> So we fix our eyes not on what is seen, but on what is unseen, since what is seen is temporary, but what is unseen is eternal. (NIV)

What does Scripture mean when it tells us to fix our eyes on what we can't even see? How do we begin to do that?

Even though as Christians we affirm the reality of the spiritual realm, sometimes we succumb to naturalistic assumptions that what we see is real and what we don't see isn't. Many people conclude that God can't be real, because we can't see Him. And Heaven can't be real, because we can't see it. But we must recognize our blindness. The blind must take by faith that there are stars in the sky. If they depend on their ability to see, they will conclude there are no stars.

Sitting here in what C. S. Lewis called the Shadowlands,

we must remind ourselves what Scripture tells us about Heaven. We will one day be delivered from the blindness that obscures the light of God's world.

For many people—including many believers—Heaven is a mysterious word describing a place that we can't understand and therefore don't look forward to. But Scripture tells us differently. What we otherwise could not have known about Heaven, God says *He has revealed to us through His Spirit* (1 Corinthians 2:10). God tells us about our eternal home in His Word, not so we can shrug our shoulders and remain ignorant, but because He wants us to anticipate what awaits us and those we love, and because *it has the power to transform the way we live today.*

Life on earth matters not because it's the only life we have, but precisely because it isn't—it's the beginning of a life that will continue without end. It's the precursor of life on the New Earth. Eternal life doesn't begin when we die; it has already begun. With eternity in view, nearly any honest activity—whether building a shed, driving a bus, pruning trees, changing diapers or caring for a patient—can be an investment in God's kingdom.

God is eternal. His Place is eternal. His Word is eternal. His people are eternal. Center your life around God, His Place, His Word, and His people, and reach out to those eternal souls who desperately long for His person and His place. Then no matter what you do for a living, your days here will make a profound difference for eternity—*and* you will be fulfilling the biblical admonition to fix your eyes on what is unseen.

This book includes 60 daily devotionals on a variety of topics related to living each day purposefully with an eternal perspective. (My thanks to Stephanie Anderson for compiling things I've written and quotations I've collected.) I hope they will encourage you to live with eternity in mind as you follow Jesus with all your heart.

—*Randy Alcorn*

Day 1

LIVING FOR
THE LINE

When we live with eternity in view, even washing dishes and repairing carburetors become an investment in God's plan.

The people who change lives are the ones who point us away from the world's short-term perspective to God's long-term perspective. Life on earth is a dot, a brief window of opportunity; life in Heaven (and ultimately on the New Earth) is a line going out from that dot for eternity. If we're smart, we'll live not for the dot, but for the line.

When we view our short today in light of eternity's long tomorrow (to use A. W. Tozer's expression), even the little choices we make become tremendously important. After death we will never have another chance to share Christ with one who can be saved, to give a cup of water to the thirsty, to serve our church. No wonder Scripture commands us, "Set your minds on things above, not on earthly things" (Colossians 3:2, NIV).

From childhood most of us learn to stifle our thirst for

the eternal, replacing it with the pursuit of the temporal. But when we live with eternity in view we'll do things with a transformed perspective—not only preaching and witnessing but also washing dishes and repairing carburetors. Almost any honest activity can be an eternal contribution, an investment in God's eternal plan.

PERSPECTIVES FROM GOD'S WORD

"If then you have been raised with Christ, seek the things that are above, where Christ is, seated at the right hand of God" (Colossians 3:1).

"And whoever gives one of these little ones even a cup of cold water because he is a disciple, truly, I say to you, he will by no means lose his reward" (Matthew 10:42).

PERSPECTIVES FROM GOD'S PEOPLE

"Let no one apologize for the powerful emphasis Christianity lays upon the doctrine of the world to come. Right there lies its immense superiority to everything else within the whole sphere of human thought or experience. ...We do well to think of the long tomorrow." —A. W. Tozer

"If you read history you will find that the Christians who did most for the present world were precisely those who thought most of the next." —C. S. Lewis

Day 2

Seeing God as the Source

We should see God as the Source of all good and *our Sustainer through everything bad. God alone is the Fountain of Life.*

We should see God everywhere in His creation: in the food we eat, the friendships we enjoy, and the pleasures of family, work, and hobbies. But we should never let these secondary pleasures eclipse our love for God (in fact, sometimes we must forgo them). We should thank Him for all of life's joys, and allow them to draw us closer to Him.

God welcomes prayers of thanksgiving for a simple meal, a lively conversation, a captivating book, and every other good thing. When we fail to acknowledge God as the Source of all good things, we fail to give Him the recognition and glory He deserves. We separate God from joy, which is like trying to separate heat from fire or wetness from rain.

We should see God as the Source of all good and our Sustainer through everything bad. Consider the perspective of one accustomed to suffering who can still say, "They feast on the abundance of your house, and you give them drink from the river of your delights. For with you is the fountain of life" (Psalm 36:8–9). God alone is the Fountain of Life. Without Him there could be neither life nor joy, neither abundance nor delights.

PERSPECTIVES FROM GOD'S WORD

"My heart exults, and with my song I give thanks to him" (Psalm 28:7).

"Every good gift and every perfect gift is from above" (James 1:17).

PERSPECTIVES FROM GOD'S PEOPLE

"There are but two lessons for Christians to learn: the one is, to enjoy God in everything; the other is, to enjoy everything in God." —Charles Simeon

"He loves Thee too little who loves anything together with Thee, which he loves not for Thy sake." —Augustine

THE PRESERVING POWER OF HUMILITY

When we become proud, we operate outside the grace God only gives to the humble. Humility preserves us; pride destroys us.

When we start thinking we're special, that we've earned people's respect, that we have a lot to offer, then we become proud. That means God is opposed to us, and we are operating outside of the grace that He only gives to the humble. That makes us a fall waiting to happen: "Pride goes before destruction and a haughty spirit before a fall" (Proverbs 16:18).

Humility preserves us; pride destroys us. Acting in arrogance is like wearing a sign that says "kick me." Being proud is a prayer to God: "strike me down." It's a prayer He's certain to answer. Every day, every hour, we choose either to humble ourselves or to be proud.

If you want to be humble, take a good look at God and then a good look at yourself, and notice the difference. When you see Him as He is and yourself as you are, the very thought of being proud or arrogant should be absolutely laughable.

PERSPECTIVES FROM GOD'S WORD

"Whoever exalts himself will be humbled, and whoever humbles himself will be exalted" (Matthew 23:12).

"Likewise, you who are younger, be subject to the elders. Clothe yourselves, all of you, with humility toward one another, for 'God opposes the proud but gives grace to the humble.' Humble yourselves, therefore, under the mighty hand of God so that at the proper time he may exalt you" (1 Peter 5:5–6).

PERSPECTIVES FROM GOD'S PEOPLE

"Let us watch against pride in every shape—pride of intellect, of wealth, of our own goodness." —J. C. Ryle

"Pride is spiritual cancer: it eats up the very possibility of love, or contentment, or even common sense." —C. S. Lewis

"They that know God will be humble; they that know themselves cannot be proud." —John Flavel

Day 4

TRUE
HAPPINESS

When I believe ultimate happiness is found only in God, then I will shut out distractions and open His Word.

If I buy into the lie that happiness is to be found in wealth, beauty, fame, or any number of endless pursuits besides Christ, I'm doomed to unhappiness because I'm pursuing the wrong things.

But when I believe that ultimate happiness and transcendent joy are to be found only in God, then I will turn off the TV and turn off talk radio and sports radio. I will back away from the Internet and video games, open the Word of God and ask His Spirit to speak joy into my life.

It takes work to set the Lord always before you and to find your happiness in Him. But when you do, the payoff is huge.

PERSPECTIVES FROM GOD'S WORD

"You satisfy me more than the richest feast. I will praise you with songs of joy" (Psalm 63:5, NLT).

"Behold, I long for your precepts; in your righteousness give me life!" (Psalm 119:40).

PERSPECTIVES FROM GOD'S PEOPLE

"To be truly happy—a man must have sources of gladness which are not dependent on anything in this world." —J. C. Ryle

"If you hope for happiness in the world, hope for it from God, and not from the world." —David Brainerd

Day 5

ONLY
ONE WAY

If I want to arrive in Heaven, I cannot go through Buddha, Mohammed or Moses. I can only go through Jesus.

You may be troubled, feeling uncertain or unready to finish this life. Make sure of your relationship with Jesus Christ. Be certain that you're trusting Him alone to save you—not anyone or anything else, and certainly not any good works you've done.

Jesus didn't say, "I am a way and a truth and a life; I'm one of the ways to come to the Father." He said, "I am THE way and the truth and the life. No one comes to the Father except through me" (John 14:6).

If I wish to fly from Portland to North Carolina I can get there a number of ways. I can fly through Denver, Minneapolis, Chicago, Detroit, Salt Lake City, Dallas or Atlanta. But if I want to arrive in Heaven, I cannot go through Buddha, Mohammed or Moses. I can only go through Jesus.

PERSPECTIVES FROM GOD'S WORD

"And there is salvation in no one else, for there is no other name under heaven given among men by which we must be saved" (Acts 4:12).

"Behold, now is the favorable time; behold, now is the day of salvation" (2 Corinthians 6:2).

PERSPECTIVES FROM GOD'S PEOPLE

"The essence of sin is man substituting himself for God, while the essence of salvation is God substituting himself for man." —John Stott

"Fallen man is not simply an imperfect creature who needs improvement: he is a rebel who must lay down his arms." —C. S. Lewis

Day 6

THE FREEDOM OF FEARING GOD

Once our sins are confessed, though we still fear God, we can come boldly before His throne.

Scripture is full of commands to fear God and it is also full of commands not to be afraid. If we fear God, we need not be afraid of anyone or anything else. But if we don't fear God, we have reason to be afraid of other things. You fear God when you come to grips with the fact that He is right and you are not, and He is in charge and you are not. "…that he may learn to fear the Lord his God" (Deuteronomy 17:19).

God is not a genie, under our control. He is the Master. When we fancy ourselves masters, it can be intimidating to agree to being a servant. Christ is in charge of the universe whether or not we recognize Him—but when we do, we honor Him by submitting to His lordship.

In many Scripture passages, God calls upon us to fear Him. But once our sins are confessed He says we can come to Him saying "Abba, Father" (meaning Papa or Daddy). We can come boldly before His throne with the access only permitted to the King's children. We still fear Him, but in a way that does not diminish our love for Him, or His for us. "Let us then with confidence draw near to the throne of grace" (Hebrews 4:16).

PERSPECTIVES FROM GOD'S WORD

"The fear of the LORD is a fountain of life, that one may turn away from the snares of death" (Proverbs 14:27).

"Only fear the LORD and serve him faithfully with all your heart. For consider what great things he has done for you" (1 Samuel 12:24).

PERSPECTIVES FROM GOD'S PEOPLE

"The fear of God is the death of every other fear; like a mighty lion, it chases all other fears before it."
—Charles Spurgeon

"We are more concerned about looking stupid (fear of people) than we are about acting sinfully (fear of the Lord)."
—Edward T. Welch

Day 7

HE IS ALWAYS SOVEREIGN

Is God sovereign only when I get my way, or is He always sovereign? The God who's sovereign in small things also controls the big ones.

The One in control of the universe has His time and place for all of us. Knowing this should help us walk by faith as we seek His face about what to do and where to go next. He is sovereign, and is not taken by surprise. He is the God of providence who raises up not just Esther, but each of us for "such a time as this" (Esther 4:14).

The true test of our belief in a sovereign God is when we have a week of rain on a long-awaited camping trip, or the washer—with our best delicate clothes in it—fills with muddy water from a broken water main (this happened to my wife Nanci). Is God sovereign when He deals with the rise and fall of empires but not when my tent leaks or my favorite shirt is ruined? Is He always sovereign or just when I get my way?

I hope you have a big view of God and His sovereignty. He is a God of all greatness. Don't underestimate Him.

PERSPECTIVES FROM GOD'S WORD

"...for I am God, and there is no other; I am God, and there is none like me" (Isaiah 46:9).

"Now to him who is able to do far more abundantly than all that we ask or think, according to the power at work within us" (Ephesians 3:20).

PERSPECTIVES FROM GOD'S PEOPLE

"The sovereignty of God is the one impregnable rock to which the suffering human heart must cling. The circumstances surrounding our lives are no accident: they may be the work of evil, but that evil is held firmly within the mighty hand of our sovereign God." —Margaret Clarkson

"Most Christians salute the sovereignty of God but believe in the sovereignty of man." —R. C. Sproul

Day 8

THE GRACE
OF GIVING

Jesus Christ is the matchless Giver. No matter how much we give, we can never out give God.

When God provides more money, we often think, "This is a blessing." Yes, but it would be just as scriptural to say, "This is a test." Abundance isn't God's provision for me to live in luxury. God entrusts me with His money not to build my kingdom on earth, but to build His kingdom in Heaven.

The act of giving is a vivid reminder that it's all about God, not about us. It's saying I am not the point, He is the point. He does not exist for me; I exist for Him. God's money has a higher purpose than my affluence. Giving affirms Christ's lordship—it dethrones me and exalts Him.

As we learn to give, we draw closer to God. But no matter how far we move on in the grace of giving, Jesus Christ remains the matchless Giver: "For you know the grace of our Lord Jesus Christ, that though he was rich, yet for your sakes he became poor, so that you through his poverty might become rich" (2 Corinthians 8:9). No matter how much we give, we can never out give God. (This is not health and wealth gospel—God gives to us in a thousand ways besides material prosperity.)

PERSPECTIVES FROM GOD'S WORD

"You will be enriched in every way so that you can be generous on every occasion" (2 Corinthians 9:11).

"Everything comes from you, and we have given you only what comes from your hand" (1 Chronicles 29:14, NIV).

PERSPECTIVES FROM GOD'S PEOPLE

"I shovel out the money, and God shovels it back—but God has a bigger shovel." — R. G. LeTourneau

"There ought to be things we should like to do and cannot because our charitable expenditure excludes them."
—C. S. Lewis

Day 9

GRASPING OUR NEED FOR GRACE

When we fail to see that we have sinned against God above all, we will inevitably minimize our sin.

The greater our grasp of our sin and alienation from God, the greater our grasp of God's grace. Charles Spurgeon put it this way: "Too many think lightly of sin, and therefore think lightly of the Saviour."

When we fail to see that we have sinned against God above all—the One who has maximum worthiness—then no matter how badly we feel about what we've done to others, we will inevitably minimize our sin.

We try to explain away sin in terms of "That's not what I meant" or "I did what my father always did to me" or "I wouldn't have done this if you hadn't done that." All these statements minimize our evil and thereby minimize the greatness of God's grace in atoning for our evil.

PERSPECTIVES FROM GOD'S WORD

"Against you, you only, have I sinned and done what is evil in your sight, so that you may be justified in your words and blameless in your judgment" (Psalm 51:4).

"Whoever conceals his transgressions will not prosper, but he who confesses and forsakes them will obtain mercy" (Proverbs 28:13).

PERSPECTIVES FROM GOD'S PEOPLE

"The thing that awakens the deepest well of gratitude in a human being is that God has forgiven sin."
—Oswald Chambers

"The beginning of the way to heaven, is to feel that we are on the way to hell." —J. C. Ryle

Day 10

HOMESICK
FOR HEAVEN

*What we really want is the person we were made for—Jesus—
and the place we were made for—Heaven. Nothing less will
satisfy.*

When I travel, I find particular joy in those places that
remind me of my lifelong home in Oregon. Likewise, one of the greatest joys that Christian pilgrims find
in this world is in those moments when it reminds them of
Heaven, their true home they've read about and dreamed
of. They live with the exhilarating assurance that at this very
moment their beloved Savior is making it ready for them.

The Bible tells us we are pilgrims, strangers, aliens and
ambassadors working far from home. Our citizenship is in
Heaven. But we've become so attached to this world that we
live for the wrong kingdom. We forget our true home, built
for us by our Bridegroom.

Nothing is more often misdiagnosed than our homesick-
ness for Heaven. We think that what we want is money, sex,

drugs, alcohol, a new job, a raise, a doctorate, a spouse, a large-screen television, a new car, a vacation. What we really want is the Person we were made for, Jesus, and the place we were made for, Heaven. Nothing less can satisfy us. "Your name and renown are the desire of our hearts" (Isaiah 26:8).

PERSPECTIVES FROM GOD'S WORD

"In my Father's house are many rooms. If it were not so, would I have told you that I go to prepare a place for you? And if I go and prepare a place for you, I will come again and will take you to myself, that where I am you may be also" (John 14:2–3).

"My desire is to depart and be with Christ, for that is far better" (Philippians 1:23).

PERSPECTIVES FROM GOD'S PEOPLE

"To come to Thee is to come home from exile, to come to land out of the raging storm, to come to rest after long labour, to come to the goal of my desires and the summit of my wishes." —Charles Spurgeon

"If I find in myself a desire which no experience in this world can satisfy, the most probable explanation is that I was made for another world." —C. S. Lewis

Day 11

PUTTING GOD'S WORD FIRST

Examine truth-claims by God's Word. Reject what doesn't sync. Don't let television news, crime shows, sitcoms or American Idol *forge your worldview.*

We should come to God's Word to examine truth-claims. If we're more eager to watch a sitcom, *American Idol*, a game, or the news than we are to read God's Word, inevitably our worldview will be influenced more by television than by God. How could it be otherwise?

As a biblical Christian, I must not only affirm the inspiration of God's Word; I must also consciously critique everything else in light of Scripture (otherwise all else will unconsciously conform my mind to the world, the flesh and the devil). I must make an effort to evaluate my beliefs and lifestyle preferences by God's Word.

As the old adage says, "If you always do what you've always done, you'll always get what you've always got." My heart and character won't change unless my daily habits change. Holy habits such as meditation, prayer, and church should be determined commitments. How we spend our time verifies what we value most: TV, the Internet, or God's Word? The fruit of the Spirit includes self-control. We already know what the world thinks—how much more do we need to hear? Choose to be in touch with the mind of God.

PERSPECTIVES FROM GOD'S WORD

"Now the Berean Jews were of more noble character than those in Thessalonica, for they received the message with great eagerness and examined the Scriptures every day to see if what Paul said was true" (Acts 17:11, NIV).

"Let the Word of Christ dwell in you richly" (Colossians 3:16).

PERSPECTIVES FROM GOD'S PEOPLE

"The new life in Christ must be nourished. This is possible only in communion with Christ and through the word of Scripture." —Herman Bavinck

"The vigor of our spiritual life will be in exact proportion to the place held by the Bible in our life and thoughts." —George Müller

Day 12

A DEMONSTRATION OF MATCHLESS LOVE

God could have created us without loving us, but He would not have gone to the Cross without loving us.

Christian love finds its pattern and origin in God. God loves us even though we are unlovable. God loves us even though we don't deserve it. We haven't earned His love. We are unworthy. This love, expressed at the cross of Jesus, is agape love, unmerited and free.

Colin S. Smith writes, "When our sin reached its full horror, God's love was displayed in all its glory. If you doubt God's love for you, look at the cross. No other love can match this. Nothing else in our experience can come close. God's love for us in Christ is greater than we ever dared to dream."

The cross of Jesus means that God, out of love, did everything for me. So why shouldn't I be willing to do anything for Him?

Perspectives from God's Word

"…but God shows his love for us in that while we were still sinners, Christ died for us" (Romans 5:8).

"…that you, being rooted and grounded in love, may have strength to comprehend with all the saints what is the breadth and length and height and depth, and to know the love of Christ that surpasses knowledge, that you may be filled with all the fullness of God" (Ephesians 3:17–19).

Perspectives from God's People

"Christians have learned that when there seems to be no other evidence of God's love, they cannot escape the cross."
—D. A. Carson

"God does something to us as well as for us through the cross. He persuades us that He loves us."
—Sinclair Ferguson

Day 13

CONTAGIOUS EXCITEMENT FOR HEAVEN

Like a bride's dreams of sharing a home with her groom, our love for Heaven should overflow and be contagious.

When I anticipate what my first glimpse of Heaven will be like, I remember the first time I went snorkeling. Etched in my memory is a certain sound—one that startled me several times, causing me to look all around me. Then I realized what it was—the sound of my own gasp going through the snorkel as I marveled at the sights. I imagine our first glimpse of Heaven will cause us to similarly gasp in amazement and delight. That first gasp will likely be followed by many more as we encounter new sights in that endlessly wonderful place.

Like a bride's dreams of sharing a home with her groom, our love for Heaven should be overflowing and contagious. The more I learn about God, the more excited I get about Heaven. The more I learn about Heaven, the more excited I get about God. Jesus said, "I am going there to prepare a place for you...I will come back and take you to be with me that you also may be where I am" (John 14:2–3, NIV).

Hope is the light at the end of life's tunnel. It not only makes the tunnel endurable, it fills the heart with anticipation of the world into which we will one day emerge. Not just a better world, but a new and perfect world. A world alive, fresh, beautiful, devoid of pain, suffering, and war, a world without earthquakes, without tsunamis, without tragedy. A world ruled by the only One worthy of ruling.

PERSPECTIVES FROM GOD'S WORD

"They desire a better country, that is, a heavenly one. Therefore God is not ashamed to be called their God, for he has prepared for them a city" (Hebrews 11:16).

"You make known to me the path of life; in your presence there is fullness of joy; at your right hand are pleasures forevermore" (Psalm 16:11).

PERSPECTIVES FROM GOD'S PEOPLE

"When Christ calls me Home I shall go with the gladness of a boy bounding away from school." —Adoniram Judson, *on his deathbed*

"Anyone who has been in foreign lands longs to return to his own native land.... We regard paradise as our native land." —Cyprian

Day 14

FORGIVENESS IS A CHOICE

Forgiveness is a matter of choice, not feelings. We demonstrate true forgiveness when we refuse to brood over the sins committed against us.

The assumption that life shouldn't be so hard leads to self-pity and endless finger-pointing. We see life as unfair and ourselves as victims, and focus on the offenses others have done against us. We fail to realize these offenses pale in comparison to our own offenses against God, who not only forgives us, but requires and enables us to forgive others and move forward free from the past.

Forgiveness is a matter of choice, not feelings. Yes, we may remember the facts, but we must not allow ourselves to dwell on them. It is possible to "forgive and forget" if we truly do forgive. But we will never forget what we choose to brood over, demonstrating that we haven't truly forgiven.

C. S. Lewis wrote, "To be a Christian means to forgive the inexcusable, because God has forgiven the inexcusable in you." Jesus said if your brother "sins against you seven times in the day, and turns to you seven times, saying, 'I repent,' you must forgive him" (Luke 17:4).

PERSPECTIVES FROM GOD'S WORD

"For if you forgive others their trespasses, your heavenly Father will also forgive you, but if you do not forgive others their trespasses, neither will your Father forgive your trespasses" (Matthew 6:14–15).

"Be kind to one another, tenderhearted, forgiving one another, as God in Christ forgave you" (Ephesians 4:32).

PERSPECTIVES FROM GOD'S PEOPLE

"As Christians we are forgiven people. We are likewise called to be forgiving people." —R. C. Sproul

"It takes two to reconcile, so it is not always possible to be reconciled. But it takes only one to forgive. So if people do you wrong, forgive them, whether or not they ask for forgiveness. You cannot cancel their sin. Only God can do that, and He will only do it if they repent. But what you can do is set aside your own anger, bitterness, and resentment towards them." —Philip Graham Ryken

SHAPING OUR WORDS AFTER HIS

To have lasting value and impact, our words must be touched and shaped by God's words.

The power of the words we speak is far greater than we realize. "Life and death is in the power of the tongue" (Proverbs 18:21).

God gives me no task except that which requires my dependence on Him to do it. Therefore, there is nothing I should regard as automatic. No conversation should be on auto-pilot. I need to ask for His guidance, His wisdom and His empowerment so my words please Him; so I will not have to account for careless words on the Day of Judgment.

If we want our words to have lasting value and impact, they need to be touched and shaped by God's words. That will happen as we make an ongoing daily choice to expose our minds to Scripture, to meet with Christ, and let Him rub off on us.

PERSPECTIVES FROM GOD'S WORD

"I tell you, on the day of judgment people will give account for every careless word they speak," (Matthew 12:36).

"So shall my word be that goes out from my mouth; it shall not return to me empty, but it shall accomplish that which I purpose, and shall succeed in the thing for which I sent it" (Isaiah 55:11).

PERSPECTIVES FROM GOD'S PEOPLE

"An unbridled tongue is the chariot of the devil, wherein he rides in triumph." —Edward Reyner

"God has given us two ears, but one tongue, to show that we should be swift to hear, but slow to speak. God has set a double fence before the tongue, the teeth and the lips, to teach us to be wary that we offend not with our tongue." —Thomas Watson

Day 16

THE MASTER ARTIST

Eden has been trampled and vacated. Nevertheless, in nature and art and music we see and hear vestiges of God's beauty and creativity.

To study creation is to study the Creator. Science should be worshipful discovery because the heavens and all creation declare God's glory (Psalm 19:1). God reveals His character in flowers, waterfalls, animals, and planets. God's name is written large in nature in His beauty, organization, skill, precision, and attention to detail. He's the Master Artist.

We're told that God's "invisible qualities" can be "clearly seen" in "what has been made" (Romans 1:20). This is God's general revelation. Eden has been trampled, torched, savaged and vacated. Nevertheless, in our own bodies and in our world we can see the intricacy of God's craftsmanship; and in flowers and rain and art and music we see and hear vestiges of God's beauty and creativity.

As a boy I had a passionate interest in astronomy. I remember vividly the thrill of first seeing Saturn's rings through my new telescope when I was eleven years old. It exhilarated me and stirred my heart. Five years later, I heard the gospel for the first time and came to know Jesus, but the wonders of the heavens helped lead me to God.

PERSPECTIVES FROM GOD'S WORD

"And God saw everything that he had made and behold, it was very good" (Genesis 1:31).

"Yours is the day, yours also the night; you have established the heavenly lights and the sun. You have fixed all the boundaries of the earth; you have made summer and winter" (Psalm 74:16–17).

PERSPECTIVES FROM GOD'S PEOPLE

"As a house implies a builder, and a garment a weaver, and a door a carpenter, so does the existence of the Universe imply a Creator." —Marquis de Vauvenargues

"The more I study nature, the more I stand amazed at the work of the Creator." —Louis Pasteur

Day 17

WHAT WE'RE REALLY LONGING FOR

We may imagine we want a thousand different things, but God is the One we really long for.

"O God, you are my God, earnestly I seek you; my soul thirsts for you, my body longs for you, in a dry and weary land where there is no water" (Psalm 63:1). We may imagine we want a thousand different things, but God is the One we really long for. His presence brings satisfaction; His absence brings thirst and longing.

Asaph says, "Whom have I in heaven but you? And earth has nothing I desire besides you" (Psalm 73:25). This may seem an overstatement—there's nothing on Earth this man desires but God? But he's affirming that the central desires of our heart are for God. No matter what we think we're searching for, God is who we truly hope to find. Augustine prayed, "You have made us for yourself, O Lord, and our hearts are restless until they rest in you."

When we see Him with our resurrected eyes, we will

realize that all our lives, as we went down every dead end street pursuing what we thought we wanted, it was really Him we were longing for.

PERSPECTIVES FROM GOD'S WORD

"As a deer pants for flowing streams, so pants my soul for you, O God. My soul thirsts for God, for the living God" (Psalm 42:1–2).

"Yet in my flesh I shall see God, whom I shall see for myself, and my eyes shall behold, and not another. My heart faints within me!" (Job 19:26–27).

PERSPECTIVES FROM GOD'S PEOPLE

"How sweet all at once it was for me to be rid of those fruitless joys which I had once feared to lose! You drove them from me, you who are the true, the sovereign joy. You drove them from me and took their place, you who are sweeter than all pleasure." —Augustine

"Christ is the desire of nations, the joy of angels, the delight of the Father. What solace then must that soul be filled with, that has the possession of Him to all eternity!"
—John Bunyan

Day 18

LISTENING TO HIS VOICE

Time spent in God's Word and prayer is never wasted—it sets our compass needle to true north.

"My sheep listen to my voice," Jesus said (John 10:27, NIV). Have you been listening to His voice lately? Have you been putting your ear to His Word and asking Him to speak to you?

I enjoy regular time with God. Some of my sweetest memories are of days given over to God—having meals with just Him, taking a long bike ride with Him, talking with Him, reading good books with Him by my side, listening to His Word and asking Him to speak to me.

There is no substitute for time spent with our Father in Heaven. Time spent in His Word and prayer is never wasted. It sets our compass needle to true north, and brings quality to all the rest of our time.

PERSPECTIVES FROM GOD'S WORD

"You will seek me and find me, when you seek me with all your heart" (Jeremiah 29:13).

"With my whole heart I seek you; let me not wander from your commandments!" (Psalm 119:10).

PERSPECTIVES FROM GOD'S PEOPLE

"We rise from the Bible ... with a knowledge of the character of God. There is a real analogy here to our relation with an earthly friend. How do we come to know one another? Not all at once, but by years of observation of one another's actions ... So it is, somewhat, with the knowledge of God that we obtain from the Bible ... by what we see we learn to know Him." —J. Gresham Machen

"One gem from that ocean is worth all the pebbles from earthly streams." —Robert Murray M'Cheyne, *speaking of the Scriptures*

SEEKING GOD'S WILL

The Bible is the revealed will of God. If you want to live in His will, then "Let the Word of Christ dwell in you richly" (Colossians 3:16).

K nowing the will of God has become much easier for me as years pass. It's not that I have to know exactly where to go, but that when I go anywhere I ask Him for direction, seek to surrender each day to Him, and ask Him to bring into my life those divine appointments that make life so interesting. God appoints the times and places we live (Acts 17:26), and is a Master of exact timing.

The Bible is the revealed will of God. If you want to live in His will, then "Let the Word of Christ dwell in you richly" (Colossians 3:16) Fill your heart and mind with the Word of God, trust in His empowerment to obey Him, and confess and repent when you disobey and fail. If you do this, you will be living in the will of God!

God's will is more than a duty; it's a joyful opportunity.

What a privilege to serve Him. I want to know Christ, like Paul said in Philippians 3. When you know Christ, when you fellowship with His people, and when you saturate yourself in His Word, knowing God's will becomes less mysterious, and doing His will tends to follow naturally (or supernaturally, depending on how you look at it).

PERSPECTIVES FROM GOD'S WORD

"May the God of peace…equip you with everything good that you may do his will, working in us that which is pleasing in his sight, through Jesus Christ" (Hebrews 13:20–21).

"Do not be conformed to this world, but be transformed by the renewal of your mind, that by testing you may discern what is the will of God" (Romans 12:2).

PERSPECTIVES FROM GOD'S PEOPLE

"Let us pray to the Lord that we may do his will on Earth as it is done in Heaven, that is, joyfully, without the slightest weariness. When our hearts are right, it is a glad thing to serve God though it be only to unloose the laces of our Master's shoes." —Charles Spurgeon

"There are two kinds of people: those who say to God, 'Thy will be done,' and those to whom God says, 'All right, then, have it your way.'" —C. S. Lewis

TRUE
REPENTANCE

To be repentant means to be committed to doing whatever is necessary to keep from falling back into sin.

Repentance is more than reciting well-calculated words while trying to minimize our losses. Genuine repentance is utterly vulnerable. It confesses more than has been found out. It never withholds information in the hope of preserving an image or a reputation. It puts itself at the mercy of others; it does not presume to direct or control them.

Psalm 51 is an expression of pure repentance. Notice there is no explanation of the extenuating circumstances—of how busy King David is, how lonely the man at the top is, how irresponsible it was for Bathsheba to be naked on a rooftop, how Uriah was a neglectful husband. David didn't explain or rationalize or justify or qualify his sin. HE OWNED UP TO IT 100%. He just admitted he was wrong.

To be repentant means to be committed to doing whatever is necessary to keep from falling back into sin. God says,

"Bear fruit in keeping with repentance" (Matthew 3:8). The sincerity of your repentance is demonstrated by how willing you are to take the steps necessary to nourish your soul and reprogram your mind from the Scriptures, so that you can draw on Christ's power to be righteous.

PERSPECTIVES FROM GOD'S WORD

"A broken and contrite heart, O God, you will not despise" (Psalm 51:17).

"Repent therefore, and turn back, that your sins may be blotted out, that times of refreshing may come from the presence of the Lord" (Acts 3:19–20).

PERSPECTIVES FROM GOD'S PEOPLE

"When our Lord and Master Jesus Christ said 'Repent,' he intended that the entire life of believers should be repentance." —Martin Luther

"The first spiritual step on the Calvary road of radical obedience to Jesus is repentance. Repentance includes remorse for inward corruption and sin. Repentance is not only remorse. It is a change of mind and heart about sin and righteousness and about Christ. It is a turning from the broken cisterns of the world to the fountain of life." —John Piper

Day 21

BREAKING OUR ADDICTION TO MATERIALISM

Even if materialism brought happiness in this life (which it certainly does not), it would leave us woefully unprepared for the next.

Materialism blinds us to our spiritual poverty. It's a fruitless attempt to find meaning outside of God, the Source of all life and the Giver of all good gifts. "For you say, I am rich, I have prospered, and I need nothing, not realizing that you are wretched, pitiable, poor, blind, and naked" (Revelation 3:17).

Seeking fulfillment in money, land, houses, cars, clothes, RVs, and vacations has left us bound and gagged by materialism—and like addicts, we think our only hope lies in getting more of the same. Meanwhile, the voice of God—unheard amid the clamor—is telling us that even if materialism did bring happiness in this life (which it doesn't), it would leave us woefully unprepared for the next.

John D. Rockefeller said, "I have made many millions,

but they have brought me no happiness." Scripture says, "Cast but a glance at riches, and they are gone, for they will surely sprout wings and fly off to the sky like an eagle" (Proverbs 23:5, NIV). What a picture! Next time you buy a prized possession, imagine it sprouting wings and flying off. Sooner or later it will disappear.

But if you've obeyed Jesus' words in Matthew 6:19–21, and stored up your treasures in Heaven, not Earth, then your treasures will last forever.

Perspectives from God's Word

"And he said to them, 'Take care, and be on your guard against all covetousness, for one's life does not consist in the abundance of his possessions'" (Luke 12:15).

"Sweet is the sleep of a laborer, whether he eats little or much, but the full stomach of the rich will not let him sleep" (Ecclesiastes 5:12).

Perspectives from God's People

"Our God is a consuming fire. He consumes pride, lust, materialism, and other sin." —Leonard Ravenhill

"He is no fool who gives what he cannot keep to gain what he cannot lose." —Jim Elliot

Day 22

THE CHRISTIAN OPTIMIST

If God is good and sits on the throne and everything that enters our life is Father-filtered, how can we be anything less than optimistic?

The only proper foundation for optimism is the redemptive work of Jesus Christ. Any other foundation is sand, not rock. It will not bear the weight of our eternity.

If we build our lives on the solid foundation of Jesus' redemptive work, we should all be optimists. Even our most painful experiences in life are temporary setbacks. No Christian should be pessimistic. We should be realists—focused on the reality that we serve a sovereign and gracious God.

If God is good and sits on the throne of the universe and everything that comes into our lives is Father-filtered... how can we be anything less than optimistic? The Christian's optimism is based squarely on realism: God is real, the atonement is real, the resurrection is real, the second coming is real, God's providence is real, and the gospel really is "good news."

PERSPECTIVES FROM GOD'S WORD

"But the Lord has become my stronghold, and my God the rock of my refuge" (Psalm 94:22).

"That through death he might destroy the one who has the power of death, that is, the devil, and deliver all those who through fear of death were subject to lifelong slavery" (Hebrews 2:14–15).

PERSPECTIVES FROM GOD'S PEOPLE

"There is a difference between tears of hope and tears of hopelessness." —Erwin Lutzer

"What is your hope? Only this—His relentless grace, boundless love, patient forgiveness and unending faithfulness." —Paul Tripp

COMING TO GRIPS WITH OUR MORTALITY

Just as birth was our ticket to this world, so death is our ticket to the next. It is less of an end than a beginning.

What do we gain if we pretend mortality isn't a fact of life? It's neither morbid nor inappropriate to speak of it. Denial of truth—not truth itself—is the breeding ground for anxiety. One of the greatest gifts you can bestow on your loved ones is the honest anticipation of reunion in the better world, the one for which we were made.

Just as birth was our ticket to this world, so death is our ticket to the next. It is less of an end than a beginning. If you were told today you would be moved from the slums to a beautiful country estate, you would not focus on the life you were ending but the life you were beginning.

Death isn't the worst that can happen to us; on the contrary, for God's children, death leads to the best.

PERSPECTIVES FROM GOD'S WORD

"But as it is, they desire a better country, that is, a heavenly one" (Hebrews 11:16).

"For to me to live is Christ, and to die is gain… My desire is to depart and be with Christ, for that is far better" (Philippians 1:21, 23).

PERSPECTIVES FROM GOD'S PEOPLE

"Let us watch the Master's call. Let us not dread the question—who next, and who next? Let none of us start back as though we hoped to linger longer than others. …Let us be willing to be dealt with just as our Lord pleases. Let no doubt intervene; let no gloom encompass us. Dying is but going home." —Charles Spurgeon

"Live in Christ, die in Christ, and the flesh need not fear death." —John Knox

Day 24

FULL OF GRACE
AND TRUTH

Truth hates sin. Grace loves sinners. Those full of grace and truth—those full of Jesus—do both.

"Hate the sin, but love the sinner." No one did either like Jesus. Truth hates sin. Grace loves sinners. Those full of grace and truth—those full of Jesus—do both. "'Then neither do I condemn you,' Jesus declared. 'Go now and leave your life of sin'" (John 8:11, NIV).

Attempts to "soften" the gospel by minimizing truth keep people from Jesus. Attempts to "toughen" the gospel by minimizing grace keep people from Jesus. It's not enough for us to offer grace or truth. We must offer both.

When we offend everybody, we've declared truth without grace. When we offend nobody, we've watered down truth in the name of grace. John 1:14 tells us Jesus came full of grace AND truth. Let's not choose between them, but be characterized by both.

PERSPECTIVES FROM GOD'S WORD

"And the Word became flesh and dwelt among us, and we have seen his glory, glory as of the only Son from the Father, full of grace and truth" (John 1:14).

"For the law was given through Moses; grace and truth came through Jesus Christ" (John 1:17).

PERSPECTIVES FROM GOD'S PEOPLE

"The ultimate test of our spirituality is the measure of our amazement at the grace of God." —D. Martyn Lloyd-Jones

"True happiness is to rejoice in the truth, for to rejoice in the truth is to rejoice in You, O God, who are the truth." —Augustine

Day 25

AWAITING HEAVEN ON THE (NEW) EARTH

In the end Christ will finally and completely restore His entire creation to what God originally intended.

Utopian idealists who dream of mankind creating "Heaven on Earth" are destined for disappointment. But though their belief that humans can achieve perfection is mistaken, one day there *will* be Heaven on Earth. That's God's dream. It's God's plan. And He—not we—will accomplish it. "Now the dwelling of God is with men, and he will live with them" (Revelation 21:3).

If I promised you a new car, would you say, "If it's new, it probably won't have an engine, a transmission, doors, wheels, or windows"? No, you'd never make such assumptions. Why? Because if a new car didn't have these things, it wouldn't be a car. Likewise, when Scripture speaks of a new Earth (2 Peter 3, and Revelation 21), we can expect that it will be a far better version of the old Earth, but it will truly be Earth.

Earth can be delivered only by being resurrected. The removal of the Curse will be as thorough and sweeping as the redemptive work of Christ. In bringing us salvation, Christ has already undone some of the damage in our hearts, but in the end He'll finally and completely restore His entire creation to what God originally intended.

Perspectives from God's Word

"But according to his promise we are waiting for new heavens and a new earth in which righteousness dwells" (2 Peter 3:13).

"The creation itself will be set free from its bondage to corruption and obtain the freedom of the glory of the children of God" (Romans 8:21).

Perspectives from God's People

"We are earthlings. We were made to live here. This world is our home. For too long, many evangelical Christians have mistakenly believed that the goal of life is to escape the bounds of earth…heaven is merely the first leg of a journey that is round-trip." —Michael Wittmer

"Our destiny is an earthly one: a new earth, an earth redeemed and transfigured. An earth reunited with heaven, but an earth, nevertheless." —Paul Marshall

Day 26

EMPOWERED
FOR HOLINESS

*What an encouragement to know that even if no one else knows
our needs and is praying for us, Christ does and is.*

Don't forget that "the one [Christ] who is in you is
greater than the one who is in the world" (1 John 4:4).
As powerful as the evil one is to tempt us, God is infinitely
more powerful to deliver us and has given us in Christ all
the resources we need to live godly lives.

"Be holy for I am holy." God is the reason we should be
holy. But He's also the empowerment for our holiness. Many
of us are convinced we should be more holy, but we've gone
about it wrong. To be holy in our strength, and for our glory,
is to be distinctly unholy. To be holy in Christ's strength and
for His glory...that's our calling, and our joy.

Christ intercedes for us (Romans 8:34) for the same
reason we intercede for each other—we need help and we
need God's power to resist temptation and live holy lives.
Since the prayers of a righteous man are effective (James

5:16, NIV), what could be more effective than Christ's prayers for us? What an encouragement to know that even if no one else knows our needs and is praying for us, Christ does and is.

PERSPECTIVES FROM GOD'S WORD

"For the grace of God has appeared, bringing salvation for all people, training us to renounce ungodliness and worldly passions, and to live self-controlled, upright, and godly lives in the present age" (Titus 2:11–12).

"His divine power has granted to us all things that pertain to life and godliness" (2 Peter 1:3).

PERSPECTIVES FROM GOD'S PEOPLE

"The Spirit's work is not to make us holy, in order that we may be pardoned; but to show us the cross, where the pardon is to be found by the unholy; so that having found the pardon there, we may begin the life of holiness to which we are called." —Horatius Bonar

"Lord, make me as holy as it is possible for a saved sinner to be." —Robert Murray M'Cheyne

Day 27

A THEOLOGY
OF LAUGHTER

Who is the most intelligent, creative, witty, and joyful human being in the universe? Jesus Christ.

Often we think of ourselves as fun-loving, and of God as a humorless killjoy. But we've got it backward. We are the boring ones, not God. Did we invent wit, humor, and laughter? No. God did. We'll never begin to exhaust God's sense of humor and His love for pleasure-filled joy. "You make known to me the path of life; in your presence there is fullness of joy; at your right hand are pleasures forevermore" (Psalm 16:11).

For Nanci and me, laughter is therapy. We love to laugh. As people instinctively blink to get something out of their eye, we laugh to lighten our hearts. Have you ever laughed so hard it brought tears to your eyes? I think Christ will laugh with us, and His wit and fun-loving nature will be our greatest source of endless laughter. We need a biblical theology of humor that prepares us for an eternity of celebration and spontaneous laughter.

Who is the most intelligent, creative, witty, and joyful human being in the universe? Jesus Christ. Whose laughter will be loudest and most contagious on the New Earth? Jesus Christ's.

PERSPECTIVES FROM GOD'S WORD

"[God] will yet fill your mouth with laughter, and your lips with shouting" (Job 8:21).

"Blessed are you who weep now, for you shall laugh" (Luke 6:21).

"Well done, good and faithful servant…Enter into the joy of your master" (Matthew 25:23).

PERSPECTIVES FROM GOD'S PEOPLE

"Our sense of humor is a gift from God which should be controlled as well as cultivated." —J. Oswald Sanders

"Let it not be imagined that the life of a good Christian must be a life of melancholy and gloominess; for he only resigns some pleasures to enjoy others infinitely better."
—Blaise Pascal

Day 28

DEFEATING LUST, FEEDING RIGHT PASSIONS

We become what we choose to daily take into our minds.

God made a universe in which righteousness is always rewarded, and unrighteousness is always punished. Purity is always smart; impurity is always stupid. If we plant purity today, we will reap a rich harvest.

The problem isn't passion, but lust. We serve a passionate God. We should love and serve Him passionately. But we need to cultivate our passion for the right objects, not the wrong ones. "Each of you should learn to control his own body" (1 Thessalonians 4:4, NIV) means self-control doesn't come naturally—it requires training and discipline.

Lust is fed by whatever we've deposited in our brains that it can get its claws on. The kind of person we are becoming is determined by what we choose daily to take into our minds. When we read Scripture and good books, participate in godly discussion, or care for the needy, we are inclining ourselves toward righteousness. "For out of the heart come evil thoughts, murder, adultery, sexual immorality…" (Matthew 15:19).

PERSPECTIVES FROM GOD'S WORD

"I the Lord search the heart and test the mind, to give every man according to his ways, according to the fruit of his deeds" (Jeremiah 17: 10).

"Put to death therefore what is earthly in you: sexual immorality, impurity, passion, evil desire, and covetousness…" (Colossians 3:5).

PERSPECTIVES FROM GOD'S PEOPLE

"Saving grace makes a man as willing to leave his lusts as a slave is willing to leave his galley, or a prisoner his dungeon, or a thief his bolts, or a beggar his rags." —Thomas Brooks

"Imagination is a God-given gift; but if it is fed dirt by the eye, it will be dirty. All sin, not least sexual sin, begins with the imagination. Therefore what feeds the imagination is of maximum importance in the pursuit of kingdom righteousness." —D. A. Carson

DELIGHTING
IN HIM

Time with God is the fountain from which holiness, joy, and delight flow. It reminds us who we are and whose we are.

Have you been sitting at the feet of Jesus, as Mary of Bethany did (Luke 10:38–42)? Have you been turning your back on a thousand distractions to enjoy the presence of your Bridegroom, the Carpenter from Nazareth—the One who said He was going to prepare a place for you and is coming back to get you so you can be with Him forever?

Time with God is the fountain from which holiness flows … and joy, and delight. It reminds us who we are … and whose we are. Our citizenship is in Heaven (Philippians 3:20). We are "foreigners and strangers on earth," who are "longing for a better country—a heavenly one" (Hebrews 11:13–16, NIV).

If we delight ourselves in God, that will transform the desires of our hearts. We will want what He wants. We will want His closeness, and the desire of our hearts will be to hear Him say to us, "Well done." And when that day comes He will flood us with more joy that we can imagine. He will say, "Enter into the joy of your master" (Matthew 25:21, 23).

PERSPECTIVES FROM GOD'S WORD

"I long for your salvation, O LORD, and your law is my delight" (Psalm 119:174).

"Delight yourself in the LORD, and he will give you the desires of your heart" (Psalm 37:4).

PERSPECTIVES FROM GOD'S PEOPLE

"God's greatest interest is to glorify the wealth of His grace by making sinners happy in Him." —John Piper

"God cannot give us happiness apart from Himself, because there is no such thing." —C. S. Lewis

Day 30

HE SUFFERED
THE MOST

Isn't it astonishing that God would willingly, premeditatedly create a world in which no one would suffer more than He?

In this world of suffering and evil, I have a profound and abiding hope, and faith for the future—not because I follow a set of religious rules to make me better, but because for forty years I've known a real Person, and today I know Him better than ever. Through inconceivable self-sacrifice He has touched me deeply, given me a new heart, and utterly transformed my life.

Some people can't believe God would create a world in which people would suffer so much. Isn't it astonishing that God would create a world in which no one would suffer more than He? That God did this willingly, with ancient premeditation, is even more remarkable.

Whenever you feel tempted to ask God, "Why did you do this to me?" look at the cross and ask, "Why did you do that *for* me?"

Perspectives from God's Word

"…I lay down my life for the sheep. …No one takes it from me, but I lay it down of my own accord" (John 10:15, 18).

"Therefore I will divide him a portion with the many, and he shall divide the spoil with the strong, because he poured out his soul to death and was numbered with the transgressors; yet he bore the sin of many, and makes intercession for the transgressors" (Isaiah 53:12).

Perspectives from God's People

"Whenever anything disagreeable or displeasing happens to you, remember Christ crucified and be silent."
—John of the Cross

"Cast your arms around the cross of Christ, and give up your heart to God, and then, come what may, I am persuaded that 'Neither death, nor life, nor angels, nor principalities, nor powers, nor things present, nor things to come. Nor height, nor depth, nor any other creature, shall be able to separate us from the love of God, which is in Christ Jesus our Lord.'" —Charles Spurgeon

Day 31

LET'S BE GRATEFUL

If only we could see our situation clearly. Anything less than gratitude? Unthinkable! He owes us nothing. We owe Him everything.

The Word of God is a corrective to the spirit of entitlement and ingratitude that's poisoning our culture, and too often the church as well. We are never grateful for what we think we deserve. On the contrary, we gripe and complain and think God and others are unfair if it doesn't come to us.

If only we could see our situation clearly—even for a moment. We deserve expulsion; He gives us a diploma. We deserve the electric chair; He gives us a parade. Anything less than overwhelming gratitude should be unthinkable. He owes us nothing. We owe Him everything.

Perhaps parents' greatest heritage to pass on to their children is the ability to perceive the multitude of God's daily blessings and to respond with continual gratitude. We should be "abounding in thanksgiving" (Colossians 2:7).

PERSPECTIVES FROM GOD'S WORD

"...giving thanks to the Father, who has qualified you to share in the inheritance of the saints in light. He has delivered us..." (Colossians 1:12–13).

"Give thanks in all circumstances..." (1 Thessalonians 5:18).

PERSPECTIVES FROM GOD'S PEOPLE

"Gratitude is not just for private consumption, but for public conversation." —Nancy Leigh DeMoss

"I would maintain that thanks are the highest form of thought; and that gratitude is happiness doubled by wonder." —G. K. Chesterton

Day 32

HUMBLE SERVANT, KNOWN BY GOD

God will evaluate our service for Him now on Earth to determine how we'll serve Him on the New Earth.

We say we want to be God's servants, and to serve others. Yet there's nothing we resent more than being treated like servants. May God give us the heart of a faithful servant, who is first about God, second about others, and third about ourselves.

Scripture teaches that God will evaluate our service for Him on the present Earth to determine how we'll serve Him on the New Earth. The humble servant will be put in charge of much, whereas the one who has lorded it over others in the present world will have power taken away: "Everyone who exalts himself will be humbled, and he who humbles himself will be exalted" (Luke 14:11).

Being well-known here doesn't matter. Hearing God say "Well done" does! To be known by God—it doesn't get any better than that!

Perspectives from God's Word

"For even the Son of Man did not come to be served but to serve, and to give his life as a ransom for many" (Mark 10:45).

"His master said to him, 'Well done, good and faithful servant. You have been faithful over a little; I will set you over much. Enter into the joy of your master'" (Matthew 25:21).

Perspectives from God's People

"Christ's followers cannot expect better treatment in the world than their Master had. Let them not promise themselves more honor or pleasure in the world than Christ had. Let each live a life of labor and self-denial as his Master, and make himself a servant of all; let him stoop, and let him toil, and do all the good he can, and then he will be a complete disciple." —Matthew Henry

"Where Jesus does not shine the soul is sick. Bask in His beams and you shall be vigorous in the service of the Lord." —Charles Spurgeon

Day 33

PRAYER: MAKING AN ETERNAL DIFFERENCE

We pray, believing our prayers are making an eternal difference; we anticipate Heaven where we'll learn God's breathtaking answers.

God's greatest works, accomplished through prayer, are often invisible to us now. We pray now in faith, believing our prayers are making an eternal difference; we anticipate Heaven, where we'll learn God's breathtaking answers to our prayers, including many that seemed unheard and ignored.

Prayer isn't passive, it's active. It's really doing something. Prayer isn't the least we can do, it's the most. "Pray in the Spirit on all occasions with all kinds of prayers and requests" (Ephesians 6:18, NIV).

James 1:5 says we don't have wisdom because we don't ask for it—so prayer is critical in seeking and living the will of God. When we are controlled by the Spirit, we won't commit the acts of the sinful nature (Galatians 5:19–21), but will produce the fruit of the Spirit (Galatians 5:22–23). When we're in God's will, we'll participate in worshipping the Lord, teaching each other, giving thanks to God, and serving others (Ephesians 5:17–33).

PERSPECTIVES FROM GOD'S WORD

"Pray without ceasing" (1 Thessalonians 5:17).

"At the beginning of your pleas for mercy a word went out" (Daniel 9:23).

PERSPECTIVES FROM GOD'S PEOPLE

"We don't believe 'in the power of prayer,' but in our all-powerful God who empowers our inherently powerless prayers." —Burk Parsons

"The Christian on his knees sees more than the philosopher on tiptoe." —D. L. Moody

Day 34

OFFERING JESUS TO THOSE WHO THIRST

In the parched wastelands of this earth, God calls us to offer refreshment—Jesus—to a world of people dying of thirst.

The world already has itself. It yearns not for what it has, but for what can come only from outside—the good news of Jesus. We proclaim "our Savior Christ Jesus, who abolished death and brought life and immortality to light through the gospel" (2 Timothy 1:10).

As long as we're still here in the parched wastelands of the present earth, God calls us to offer refreshment to a world full of people dying of thirst. What should we offer them? Exactly what they thirst for—a Person and a place. Jesus is that Person. Heaven is that place.

Have you been praying for years for someone's salvation without any visible results? Don't get discouraged. Just keep on praying, witnessing, giving them helpful books, giving of your time and affection. Be faithful to your Lord and leave the results to Him.

PERSPECTIVES FROM GOD'S WORD

"Go therefore and make disciples of all nations" (Matthew 28:19).

"And let us not grow weary of doing good, for in due season we will reap, if we do not give up" (Galatians 6:9).

PERSPECTIVES FROM GOD'S PEOPLE

"The Christian is a person who makes it easy for others to believe in God." —Robert Murray M'Cheyne

"We know but little of true Christianity, if we do not feel a deep concern about the souls of unconverted people." —J. C. Ryle

Day 35

THE AUDIENCE OF ONE

Jesus is the Audience of One. Let's live for the applause of God, not for the praise of men.

We should do what we believe pleases our Lord, regardless of how it pans out in opinion polls. That includes loving others and giving radically, ministering to the down and out and addressing addictions, and saying we think it's wrong to kill children of all ages, including the unborn. We do such things, not seeking the approval of our culture, but of our King, entrusting ourselves "to him who judges justly" (1 Peter 2:23).

Paul said, "If I were still trying to please man, I would not be a servant of Christ" (Galatians 1:10). Jesus is the Audience of One. We will stand before His judgment seat, no one else's. We should long to hear Him say, "Well done, good and faithful servant." Live for the approval of others and you will not live for Christ's approval, and therefore you will not endure.

John Chrysostom, the church father, said, "Men who

are in love with applause have their spirits starved not only when they are blamed offhand, but even when they fail to be constantly praised." It was said of some religious leaders that "they loved human praise more than praise from God" (John 12:43, NIV). Let's live our lives not for the praise of men, but for the applause of God, the Audience of One.

PERSPECTIVES FROM GOD'S WORD

"So whether we are at home or away, we make it our aim to please him" (2 Corinthians 5:9).

"Whatever you do, work heartily, as for the Lord and not for men, knowing that from the Lord you will receive the inheritance as your reward. You are serving the Lord Christ" (Colossians 3:23–24).

PERSPECTIVES FROM GOD'S PEOPLE

"Now think, my brother, you will be in Heaven very soon. Since last year a great number have gone home: before next year many more will have ascended to glory. Sitting up in those celestial seats, how shall we wish that we had lived below?" —Charles Spurgeon

"The beginning of true nobility comes when a man ceases to be interested in the judgment of men and becomes interested in the judgment of God." —J. Gresham Machen

Day 36

GOD'S GLORY,
OUR GOOD

We think God calls us to do things that won't be good for us. In fact, that which is for God's glory is for our good.

Satan has conned many Christians into a view of the Christian life that makes us imagine God calls us to do things that won't be good for us (while the unbelievers are out there having all the fun). In fact, that which is for God's glory is for our good.

Choosing what is good and right will always be to our advantage. Wrongdoing sometimes appears to offer benefits, and doing right may seem to bring serious disadvantages. But in the long run, in this life and in the afterlife, God rewards his children's right choices and confers consequences (not eternal punishment) for wrong ones. "A man reaps what he sows" (Galatians 6:7, NIV).

What is in God's best interests is also in others' best interests and in my best interests (not necessarily immediately, but always ultimately). Something that is good will be good for everyone—not good for God and bad for me, or good for me and bad for my neighbor. What's good is good for all. Every time I obey God, I'm doing what's ultimately best for all.

PERSPECTIVES FROM GOD'S WORD

"I call heaven and earth to witness against you today, that I have set before you life and death, blessing and curse. Therefore choose life, that you and your offspring may live" (Deuteronomy 30:19).

"For the simple are killed by their turning away, and the complacency of fools destroys them; but whoever listens to me will dwell secure and will be at ease, without dread of disaster" (Proverbs 1:32–33).

PERSPECTIVES FROM GOD'S PEOPLE

"God has not created a universe where you must choose between your joy and his glory." —John Piper

"Since man was made for the glory of God, he can never be what he was intended to be until his life is properly focused on the glory of God...So God's glory does not detract from man's life. Instead, His glory is the sun around which the whole of life must revolve if there is to be the light and life of God in our experience." —Sinclair Ferguson

Day 37

THE INCOMPARABLE
BEAUTY OF PURITY

*To embrace purity is to lay claim to a magnificent gift. Purity is
a beauty that will never end.*

Sexual purity is not an option for an obedient Christian—it's a requirement. God's will is centered on our character and moral purity much more than on our circumstances, such as job, housing and schooling. You want to know God's will? You don't have to wonder: "It is God's will that you should be sanctified: that you should avoid sexual immorality" (1 Thessalonians 4:3, NIV).

When God calls on you to pursue purity, you are not being asked to do what will deprive you of joy. In fact, you are being called on to do what will bring you the greatest joy!

To embrace purity is to lay claim to a magnificent gift. Purity is incomparably beautiful, like the fragrance of a rose after a summer shower. And it's a beauty that will never end, because all who live in Heaven will be pure: "Nothing impure will ever enter it, nor will anyone who does what is shameful or deceitful but only those whose names are written in the Lamb's book of life" (Revelation 21:27, NIV).

Perspectives from God's Word

"The fear of the LORD is a fountain of life, that one may turn away from the snares of death" (Proverbs 14:27).

"Put to death therefore what is earthly in you: sexual immorality, impurity, passion, evil desire, and covetousness, which is idolatry. On account of these the wrath of God is coming. In these you too once walked, when you were living in them. But now you must put them all away: anger, wrath, malice, slander, and obscene talk from your mouth" (Colossians 3:5–8).

Perspectives from God's People

"Either sin will keep you from the Word, or the Word will keep you from sin." —John Bunyan

"Little souls make little lusts have great power. The soul, as it were, expands to encompass the magnitude of its treasure. The human soul was made to see and savor the supremacy of Christ. Nothing else is big enough to enlarge the soul as God intended and make little lusts lose their power." —John Piper

Day 38

GIVING OUR BURDENS TO HIM

Many hear God say, "Do more," not, "I've done it for you—
rest." Yet Jesus said, "My yoke is easy and My burden is light."

Sometimes, in moments of pride, we need to fear God and repent. Other times, in moments of brokenness and despair, we need to just bathe in His grace, and see His smile and hear Him say "Well done, enter into your Master's joy." We need to cast our cares upon Him, because He cares for us, and come to Him when we're weary and heavy laden, and He will give us rest.

I learned years ago that I have to say no to the great majority of things I'm asked to do, so I'm available to say yes to those few God wants me to do. Jesus calls upon us to carry our crosses, yet paradoxically promises a light burden and rest for our souls. If the burden's usually heavy and our souls aren't at rest … we're missing something.

Many hear God say, "Do more" and "Do better." But not, "I've done it for you—rest." Yet this is what Jesus meant when He said, "Come to me, all who labor and are heavy laden…Take My yoke upon you, and learn from Me…For My yoke is easy and My burden is light" (Matthew 11:28–30).

PERSPECTIVES FROM GOD'S WORD

"Cast your burden on the LORD, and he will sustain you; he will never permit the righteous to be moved" (Psalm 55:22).

"For God alone my soul waits in silence; from him comes my salvation" (Psalm 62:1).

PERSPECTIVES FROM GOD'S PEOPLE

"I'm convinced that one of the major reasons we can't handle the demands of day-to-day living is that our *spirits* are weary. Our *souls* need to be restored…. The restoration of our souls is a ministry of our Great Shepherd…. If I don't take time to get my spiritual tank refilled, I soon find myself 'running on fumes.'" —Nancy Leigh DeMoss

"The eternal rest of the Gospel is this—God's affection for you isn't rooted in your performance, but in Christ's." —Paul Tripp

Day 39

GOOD WORKS AND GOD'S GLORY

Our Lord applauds righteous works done for the right reasons, for His glory and not ours.

In Revelation 19:7 we're told "'The wedding of the Lamb has come, and his bride has made herself ready. Fine linen, bright and clean, was given her to wear.' (Fine linen stands for the righteous acts of the saints.)" Note the parenthetical statement in the verse. I once cited this verse in a book and the editor "corrected" it, assuming it was my interpretation. It didn't sound right. But it is—it's Scripture!

Somewhere we've gotten the erroneous idea that to God "works" is a dirty word. This is totally false. While He condemns works done to earn salvation, and works done to impress others, our Lord enthusiastically *commends* righteous works done for the right reasons, for His glory, not for ours.

God created us to do good works, has a lifetime of good works for each of us to do, and will reward us according to whether or not we do them. Indeed, Scripture ties God's reward-giving to His very character: "God is not unjust; he will not forget your work and the love you have shown him as you have helped his people and continue to help them" (Hebrews 6:10, NIV).

PERSPECTIVES FROM GOD'S WORD

"Let your light shine before others, so that they may see your good works and give glory to your Father who is in heaven" (Matthew 5:16).

"For by grace you have been saved through faith. And this is not your own doing; it is the gift of God, not a result of works, so that no one may boast. For we are his workmanship, created in Christ Jesus for good works, which God prepared beforehand, that we should walk in them" (Ephesians 2:8–10).

PERSPECTIVES FROM GOD'S PEOPLE

"Truly, if faith is there, the believer cannot hold back … he breaks out into good works." —Martin Luther

"If we had choice of a sphere in which we could serve God with widest range, we should choose not Heaven but Earth. There are no slums and over-crowded rooms in Heaven to which we can go with help, but there are plenty of them here." —Charles Spurgeon

Day 40

THINKING LIKE
STEWARDS, NOT OWNERS

If God owns it all, shouldn't we regularly ask Him, "What do you want me to do with your money and possessions?"

When it comes to money and possessions, whenever we think like owners, it's a red flag. We should be thinking like stewards, investment managers, always looking for the best place to invest the Owner's money. At the end of our term of service, we'll undergo a job performance evaluation: "Each of us will give an account of himself to God" (Romans 14:12).

If we really believe God is the owner of all that has been entrusted to us, shouldn't we regularly ask Him, "What do you want me to do with Your money and Your possessions?" And shouldn't we be open to the possibility that He may want us to share large portions of His assets with those in need?

Jesus made a direct connection between our present handling of earthly wealth and his future decision to entrust to our care another kind of wealth. "If you are untrustworthy about worldly wealth, who will trust you with the true riches of heaven?" (Luke 16:11, NLT). There is a direct connection between our faithful use of money here and now and the "true riches" God will put us over in His future Kingdom.

PERSPECTIVES FROM GOD'S WORD

"As for the rich in this present age...they are to do good, to be rich in good works, to be generous and ready to share" (1 Timothy 6:17–18).

"'It is more blessed to give than to receive'" (Acts 20:35).

PERSPECTIVES FROM GOD'S PEOPLE

"Find out how much God has given you and from it take what you need; the remainder is needed by others."
—Augustine

"Let us walk as *stewards* and not act as owners, keeping for ourselves the means with which the Lord has entrusted us. He has not blessed us that we may gratify our own carnal mind but for the sake of using our money in His service and to His praise." —George Müller

Day 41

WHEN IT COMES TO
HEAVEN, DREAM BIG

As we get older, our childhood dreams shrink as reality sinks in. But when the Curse is reversed, our greatest dreams will be revived and lived out.

Those who know God and believe His promise of bodily resurrection can dream great dreams: Skydiving without a parachute? Maybe. Scuba diving without an air tank? I hope so. Will we be able to tolerate diving hundreds of feet without special equipment? We know that our resurrection bodies will be superior. Won't it be fantastic to test their limits? One day we will live our dreams, with Jesus.

When we're young, we dream of becoming astronauts or athletes. As we get older, our dreams shrink and "realism" sinks in. When the Curse is reversed, our dreams will be revived, enhanced and lived out. Perhaps that's part of why childlikeness is necessary for Heaven. "Let the little children come to me … for the kingdom of heaven belongs to such as these" (Matthew 19:14, NIV).

"No longer will there be any curse" (Revelation 22:3, NIV). The hope, the promise, the anticipation of this verse is inexpressible—it is weighty, thick with promise and joy. Let your imagination go where this verse leads you. Write it down, post it on your refrigerator and dashboard and bathroom mirror.

PERSPECTIVES FROM GOD'S WORD

"Beloved, we are God's children now, and what we will be has not yet appeared; but we know that when he appears we shall be like him, because we shall see him as he is" (1 John 3:2).

"But our citizenship is in heaven, and from it we await a Savior, the Lord Jesus Christ, who will transform our lowly body to be like his glorious body, by the power that enables him even to subject all things to himself" (Philippians 3:20–21).

PERSPECTIVES FROM GOD'S PEOPLE

"However miserable, powerless and contemptible in life and death [our bodies are], Christ will at his coming render our bodies beautiful, pure, shining and worthy of honor, until they correspond to his own immortal, glorious body." —Martin Luther

"The best is yet to be." —John Wesley

Day 42

KEEPING THE RIGHT PERSPECTIVE IN SUFFERING

If we have an eternal future as resurrected people living under King Jesus, no present suffering will prove worthless.

A right attitude carries you through bad circumstances and poor health. But no matter how strong the body, how positive the circumstances, a crushed spirit will never experience joy. Perspective is what makes the spirit soar like an eagle even when the body is ravaged by accident, disease, and age.

If we have no eternal future as resurrected people living under the benevolent rule of King Jesus, then our present sufferings will ultimately be worth nothing. If we have such a future, however, then no present suffering—regardless of its scope—will prove worthless. In fact, such sufferings are a means to an end: incalculable future goodness.

Shouldn't we suppose that many of our most painful ordeals will look quite different a million years from now, as we recall them on the New Earth? What if one day we discover that God has wasted nothing in our life on Earth? What if we see that every agony was part of giving birth to an eternal joy?

PERSPECTIVES FROM GOD'S WORD

"For this light momentary affliction is preparing for us an eternal weight of glory beyond all comparison" (2 Corinthians 4:17).

"For I consider that the sufferings of this present time are not worth comparing with the glory that is to be revealed to us" (Romans 8:18).

PERSPECTIVES FROM GOD'S PEOPLE

"I want to stay in the habit of 'glancing' at my problems and 'gazing' at my Lord." —Joni Eareckson Tada

"There are rare and wonderful species of joy that flourish only in the rainy atmosphere of suffering." —John Piper

Day 43

A Passion to Know the King of Kings

Don't let life just happen to you—choose to invest it in what matters.

We tend to be passionate about things that don't matter, fanatics and fans about what won't last. But we are afraid to look like fanatics for Jesus. We seem determined to portion Jesus out in acceptable portions, unwilling to appear fools for Christ. John Wesley was asked about the key to his ministry. He supposedly said, "I ask God to set me on fire and let people watch me burn."

I thank God that today I don't just love Jesus as much as I used to, I love Him more. That is to His credit, and I'm deeply grateful. He's what makes it so exciting and so worthwhile, and He's the one who empowers me to walk "a long obedience in the same direction." More than ever, I want to know Christ. How about you?

Give Jesus first place in your life. Don't just let your life happen to you—choose what to do with it or in the end you'll wonder where it went. If you're going to persevere as Christ's follower, you must consciously choose not to squander your life or let it idle away, but to invest it in what matters. "Look carefully then how you walk, not as unwise but as wise, making the best use of the time" (Ephesians 5:15).

PERSPECTIVES FROM GOD'S WORD

"I want to know Christ—yes, to know the power of his resurrection and participation in his sufferings" (Philippians 3:10, NIV).

"In your presence there is fullness of joy" (Psalm 16:11).

PERSPECTIVES FROM GOD'S PEOPLE

"The Fort Knox of faith is Christ. Fellowshipping with him. Walking with him. Pondering him. Exploring him. The heart-stopping realization that in him you are part of something ancient, endless, unstoppable, and unfathomable."
—Max Lucado

"The longer you know Christ, and the nearer you come to him, still the more do you see of his glory. Every farther prospect of Christ entertains the mind with a fresh delight. He is as it were a new Christ every day—and yet the same Christ still." —John Flavel

Day 44

THE ONE IN CHARGE

The God of providence weaves together millions of details into our lives. His thoughts and ways are far above ours.

We are not the cosmic center—God is. He holds the universe, and each of us, in His gravity. When we make ourselves the center of gravity, we attempt to hold God in orbit around us. Then we draw false conclusions, including, whenever we don't get our way, it must mean God isn't really there.

God is the source of all good and the standard by which good is measured. We may not like what God does, but we're in no position to accuse him of wrongdoing. Every breath He gives us is a gift. But if you want to hear Him say He cares about you, and sympathizes with you, listen to what He says to His people: "As a father shows compassion to his children, so the LORD shows compassion to those who fear him" (Psalm 103:13).

The God of providence weaves millions of details into

our lives and the lives around us. Maybe He doesn't have one big reason for bringing a certain person, success, failure, disease or accident into our lives; God may have hundreds of little reasons. In order to understand His explanations, we'd have to be God. "'For my thoughts are not your thoughts, neither are your ways my ways,' declares the LORD" (Isaiah 55:8, NIV).

PERSPECTIVES FROM GOD'S WORD

"For you are great and do wondrous things; you alone are God" (Psalm 86:10).

"Who has first given to me, that I should repay him? Whatever is under the whole heaven is mine" (Job 41:11).

PERSPECTIVES FROM GOD'S PEOPLE

"What comes into our minds when we think about God is the most important thing about us." —A. W. Tozer

"He who demands a reason from God is not in a fit state to receive it." —Charles Spurgeon

Day 45

WHO YOU ARE
IN THE DARK

Character is what you are in the dark when no one but God can see you.

Image is how we look on the outside. Character is who we are in the dark when no one but God can see us. Character is who we really are. All a man's ways seem innocent to him, but motives are weighed by the Lord.

Anyone can look good in front of an audience, or even in front of their friends. It's an entirely different thing to stand naked before God, to be known as you truly are on the inside.

"His divine power has granted to us all things that pertain to life and godliness" (2 Peter 1:3–4). In light of what is ours in Christ, Peter says in verse 5 that we should "make every effort" to cultivate Christlike character and habits. So if God has already given us everything we need in Christ, shouldn't we invest our lives getting to know Him better rather than seeking fulfillment elsewhere?

Perspectives from God's Word

"All the ways of a man are pure in his own eyes, but the Lord weighs the spirit" (Proverbs 16:2).

"So then, each of us will give an account of himself to God" (Romans 14:12).

Perspectives from God's People

"When wealth is lost, nothing is lost; when health is lost, something is lost; when character is lost, all is lost."
—Billy Graham

"Character may be manifested in the great moments, but it is made in the small ones." —Phillips Brooks

Day 46

YIELDING TO THE SCULPTOR'S CHISEL

Like a master sculptor making a marble block into something magnificent, God has called us to yield ourselves to His chisel.

To produce his masterpiece, the David statue, Michelangelo chose a stone all other artists had rejected. Seeing that marble block's hidden potential, he chipped away everything that wasn't David. Now, if marble had feelings, it might have resented its sculptor. While Michelangelo may not have called upon the stone to cooperate with him, God has called us to yield ourselves by submitting to His chisel.

Jesus said in Matthew 13:43, "Then the righteous will shine like the sun in the kingdom of their Father." This transformation does not simply happen after we die. It starts here and now in this world. And suffering is the instrument. God isn't just preparing a place for us. He is preparing us for that place.

If God brought eternal joy through the suffering of Jesus, can He bring eternal joy through my present suffering, and yours? If Jesus endured his suffering through anticipating the reward of unending joy, can He empower you and me to do the same?

Perspectives from God's Word

"[Jesus] who for the joy that was set before him endured the cross, despising the shame, and is seated at the right hand of the throne of God" (Hebrews 12:2).

"And we all, with unveiled face, beholding the glory of the Lord, are being transformed into the same image from one degree of glory to another. For this comes from the Lord who is the Spirit" (2 Corinthians 3:18).

Perspectives from God's People

"Being satisfied in God (or anything) always seems easier when all is going well. But when things you love are being stripped out of your hands, then the test is real. If God remains precious in those moments, then his supreme worth shines more brightly. He is most glorified." —John Piper

"That is what mortals misunderstand. They say of some temporal suffering, 'No future bliss can make up for it,' not knowing that Heaven, once attained, will work backwards and turn even that agony into a glory. " —C. S. Lewis

Day 47

FEASTING
AND FELLOWSHIP

*I thank God for the countless believers I've never met whom He's used
to draw me to Him. One day we'll feast together on the New Earth.*

In Heaven, will we spend time with people whose lives are
recorded in Scripture and church history? No doubt. Jesus told us we'll sit at the dinner table with Abraham, Isaac,
and Jacob (Matthew 8:11). If we sit with them, we should
expect to sit with others. What do people do at dinner ta-
bles? In Middle Eastern cultures dinner was—and is—not
only about good food and drink but also a time for building
relationships, talking together, and telling stories.

Who are you looking forward to meeting when you get
to Heaven? I look forward to reconnecting with many old
friends as well as my mom and dad. I look forward to thank-
ing C. S. Lewis, Francis Schaeffer, and A. W. Tozer for how
their writings have changed me. I anticipate meeting William
Carey, Hudson Taylor, Amy Carmichael, Jim Elliot, Charles
Spurgeon, D. L. Moody, Harriet Beecher Stowe, some of the

Amistad slaves, William Wilberforce and a host of others.

I thank the Lord for the countless believers—from times and places way beyond my reach—whom God has sovereignly used to draw me to Him. I long for the day when I'll sit by them at feasts on the New Earth, where we'll look at King Jesus and celebrate His greatness and works.

PERSPECTIVES FROM GOD'S WORD

"On this mountain the LORD of hosts will make for all peoples a feast of rich food, a feast of well-aged wine" (Isaiah 25:6).

"I tell you, many will come from east and west and recline at table with Abraham, Isaac, and Jacob in the kingdom of heaven" (Matthew 8:11).

PERSPECTIVES FROM GOD'S PEOPLE

"I know that Christ is all in all; and that it is the presence of God that makes heaven to be heaven. But yet it much sweetens the thoughts of that place to me that there are there such a multitude of my most dear and precious friends in Christ." —Richard Baxter

"You'll be able to go down to the corner of Gold Street and Silver Boulevard, run into Abraham, and ask him a few questions. ...You can ask Jonah what it felt like to be swallowed by a fish and live inside of it for three days." —Tony Evans

Day 48

A HEART FOR THE POOR AND NEEDY

The Good Samaritan wasn't responsible for the plight of the wounded man, but he was responsible to love him as his neighbor.

Caring for the poor is a sobering responsibility for which we will all be held accountable. Helping the poor and homeless is not a peripheral issue. God links our efforts for the poor directly to our relationship with Him. May He one day say of us what He said of King Josiah: "He judged the cause of the poor and needy; then it was well. Is not this to know me? declares the Lord" (Jeremiah 22:16).

The Good Samaritan was not responsible for the plight of the man lying beside the road. After all, he had not robbed and brutalized him. Nonetheless, he was responsible to love his neighbor as himself. He did this not simply by refraining from hurting him, but by actively helping him. He generously used his time, energy and money to care for him. Jesus instructed us to do the same (Luke 10:30–37).

Our instinct is to give to those who will give us something in return. But Jesus told us to give to "the poor, the crippled, the lame, the blind.... Although they cannot repay you, you will be repaid at the resurrection of the righteous" (Luke 14:13–14, NIV). If we give to those who can't reward us, Christ guarantees He will personally reward us in Heaven.

PERSPECTIVES FROM GOD'S WORD

"Whoever closes his ear to the cry of the poor will himself call out and not be answered" (Proverbs 21:13).

"And the King will answer them, 'Truly, I say to you, as you did it to one of the least of these my brothers, you did it to me'" (Matthew 25:40).

PERSPECTIVES FROM GOD'S PEOPLE

"The less I spent on myself and the more I gave to others, the fuller of happiness and blessing did my soul become."
—Hudson Taylor

"Do all the good you can, by all the means you can, in all the ways you can, in all the places you can, at all the times you can, to all the people you can, as long as you ever can."
—John Wesley

Day 49

IMPERFECT CHURCH, BUT CHOSEN BRIDE

Jesus calls the church His bride. If you walk away from church, you walk away from Christ's redemptive work.

Jesus calls the church His bride. He died for her, and says that ultimately the gates of Hell won't prevail against her. If you walk away from church, you walk away from Christ's redemptive work.

I understand all the hurts people have experienced in churches. Nanci and I have endured them also. There have been a few times where I have very much wanted to walk away and just go it on my own seeking private fellowship with believers here and there. I haven't done it because I don't see the biblical liberty to do it. (And after sticking with the church, in retrospect I'm very glad I didn't leave.) The church of the New Testament is not just the universal invisible body of Christ, but actual local gatherings of imperfect people, with imperfect leaders, including elders who teach and lead, where there is actual accountability and yes, when necessary, even discipline.

There are many Christ-loving church families scattered around this country and around the world. None that are perfect, many that are seeking to honor Christ. Despite past bad experiences, I encourage people not to give up on local churches, but to find one and give themselves to serving to help it become more Christ-centered. (Our ministry has helped hundreds of people find Bible-believing churches near them. Contact us at info@epm.org if you want help.)

PERSPECTIVES FROM GOD'S WORD

"Christ loved the church and gave himself up for her" (Ephesians 5:25).

"...not neglecting to meet together, as is the habit of some, but encouraging one another, and all the more as you see the Day drawing near" (Hebrews 10:25).

PERSPECTIVES FROM GOD'S PEOPLE

"Being disconnected from the local church, for whatever reason, is a dangerous way to live...like lone sheep away from the safety of the flock and the watchful care of the shepherd, [these lone rangers] are vulnerable to predators of every sort." —Nancy Leigh DeMoss

"To gather with God's people in united adoration of the Father is as necessary to the Christian life as prayer." —Martin Luther

Day 50

THE SURE HOPE OF RESURRECTION

Our society holds to youthfulness with a white-knuckled grip. Ultimately it's all in vain. But the gospel promises us eternal youthfulness in God's presence.

In our society many people look to cosmetic surgeries, implants, and other methods to remodel their crumbling bodies. We hold to youthfulness with a white-knuckled grip. Ultimately it's all in vain. But the gospel promises us eternal health, beauty, and happiness in the presence of our God and our spiritual family. It's not ours now—but it will be, in the resurrection.

In reference to the coming resurrection, Paul wrote, "But hope that is seen is no hope at all. Who hopes for what he already has? But if we hope for what we do not yet have, we wait for it patiently" (Romans 8:24–25).To many of us, "hope" sounds wishful and tentative, but biblical hope means to anticipate with trust. We expect a sure thing, purchased on the Cross, accomplished and promised by an all-knowing God.

"Thank you for making me so wonderfully complex! Your workmanship is marvelous" (Psalm 139:14, NLT). If our fallen bodies are so marvelous, as David recognizes, how much more will we praise God for our resurrection bodies? Will our eyes be able to function alternately as telescopes and microscopes? Will we be able to see new colors? Will our sense of smell be far more acute, in a world where all smells will be good? Perhaps. I can't wait to find out!

PERSPECTIVES FROM GOD'S WORD

"O death, where is your victory?" (1 Corinthians 15:55).

"Jesus said to her, 'I am the resurrection and the life. Whoever believes in me, though he die, yet shall he live'" (John 11:25).

PERSPECTIVES FROM GOD'S PEOPLE

"Peter was made to walk on water in his old body. Imagine what Christ will enable you to do in your new one?"
—Larry Dick

"No other religion, no other philosophy promises new bodies, hearts, and minds. Only in the Gospel of Christ do hurting people find such incredible hope."
—Joni Eareckson Tada

Day 51

FINDING ULTIMATE SATISFACTION

When my thirst for joy is satisfied by Christ, sin becomes unattractive. Those who drink of Jesus are fully satisfied.

Ultimate satisfaction can be found only in God, the gracious giver of all good things. We were made for Him and we will never be satisfied with less. Coming to grips with this is one of the great keys to Christian living.

When my thirst for joy is satisfied by Christ, sin becomes unattractive. I say no to the passing pleasures of immorality, not because I don't want pleasure, but because I want true pleasure, a greater and lasting pleasure found only in Christ. Those who drink of Jesus are fully satisfied (John 6:35). I can either have my thirst quenched in Jesus, or I can plunge deeper into sin in search of what's not there.

How many times in the last 24 hours have you consciously looked to God and said something like, "Please, my Savior, help me find in You today all that my heart longs for"?

Perspectives from God's Word

"For with you is the fountain of life; in your light we see light" (Psalm 36:9).

"O God, you are my God, earnestly I seek you; my soul thirsts for you, my body longs for you, in a dry and weary land where there is no water" (Psalm 63:1).

Perspectives from God's People

"We are a long time in learning that all our strength and salvation is in God." —David Brainerd

"Many come short, being satisfied with the works of God rather than hungering for and reaching on to God Himself." —A. W. Tozer

INVESTING—NOT JUST MANAGING—TIME

Don't squander the time God has entrusted to you. C. T. Studd said, "Only one life, 'twill soon be past, only what's done for Christ will last."

We are warned not to waste our time, but we are brought up to waste our lives. "Look carefully then how you walk, not as unwise but as wise, making the best use of the time, because the days are evil" (Ephesians 5:15-16).

Look up TV, computer, sports radio, and social networking in a concordance. No place in the Bible commands us to participate in them. But plenty of places command us to be pure and a good manager of the life—time, abilities, money, and opportunities—God has entrusted to you. Don't squander your time. C. T. Studd said, "Only one life, 'twill soon be past, only what's done for Christ will last."

I've spent a lot of time talking to people who've been diagnosed with terminal diseases. These people, and their loved ones, have a sudden and insatiable interest in the afterlife. Most people live unprepared for death. But those who are wise will go to a reliable source to investigate what's on the other side. They'll adjust accordingly the choices they make during their brief stay in this world.

PERSPECTIVES FROM GOD'S WORD

"So teach us to number our days that we may get a heart of wisdom" (Psalm 90:12).

"Walk in wisdom toward outsiders, making the best use of the time" (Colossians 4:5).

PERSPECTIVES FROM GOD'S PEOPLE

"Wasting time is unbecoming of a saint who is bought by the precious blood of Jesus. His time and all he has is to be used for the Lord." —George Müller

"It is impossible for a believer, no matter what his experience, to keep right with God if he will not take the trouble to spend time with God. Spend plenty of time with him; let other things go, but don't neglect Him."
—J. Oswald Sanders

THE BRIEF WINDOW OF THIS PRESENT LIFE

Many Christians think and act as if there's no eternity—we major in the momentary and minor in the momentous.

Earth is an in-between world touched by both Heaven and Hell. Earth leads directly into Heaven or directly into Hell, affording a choice between the two. The best of life on Earth is a glimpse of Heaven; the worst of life is a glimpse of Hell. For Christians, this present life is the closest they will come to Hell. For unbelievers, it is the closest they will come to Heaven.

Many Western Christians habitually think and act as if there is no eternity. We major in the momentary and minor in the momentous. What does God have to say about our lives here? He says this life is so brief we're like grass that grows up in the morning and wilts in the afternoon (Isaiah 40:6-8). Our life here is but "mist that appears for a little time and then vanishes" (James 4:14).

Are you ALIVE? (Always Living In View of Eternity)?

Are you fixing your eyes on the unseen, not the seen? (See 2 Corinthians 4:18.)

PERSPECTIVES FROM GOD'S WORD

"All flesh is grass, and all its beauty is like the flower of the field. The grass withers, the flower fades" (Isaiah 40:6–7).

"What is your life? For you are a mist that appears for a little time and then vanishes" (James 4:14).

PERSPECTIVES FROM GOD'S PEOPLE

"Two seconds and we will be gone. To heaven or to hell. Life is a vapor." —John Piper

"A man's greatest care should be for that place where he dwelleth longest; therefore eternity should be in his scope." —Thomas Manton

Day 54

THE GIFT
OF TRUTH

Truth matters because it is bigger than we are. God's Word is the truth that sets us free.

The greatest kindness we can offer each other is the truth. Our job is not just to help each other feel good but to help each other be good. We often seem to think that our only options are to: 1) speak the truth hurtfully; or 2) remain silent in the name of grace. Both are lies. Jesus came full of grace AND truth (John 1:14). We should not choose between them, but do both.

Aleksandr Solzhenitsyn said in his Nobel Prize acceptance address, "One word of truth outweighs the entire world." What did he mean? That the truth is bigger than we are. Just as the Berlin Wall finally toppled, the weight of all the world's lies can be toppled by a single truth. Truth resonates in the human heart. People may resist it, yet it's the truth they need, for it's the truth that sets them free.

God promises that His Word "will not return to me

empty, but will accomplish what I desire and achieve the purpose for which I sent it" (Isaiah 55:11, NIV). As you go through life, don't let your feelings—real as they are—invalidate your need to let the truth of God's words guide your thinking. Remember that the path to your heart travels through your mind. Truth matters.

PERSPECTIVES FROM GOD'S WORD

"You will know the truth, and the truth will set you free" (John 8:32).

"Sanctify them in the truth; your word is truth" (John 17:17).

PERSPECTIVES FROM GOD'S PEOPLE

"Christ's people must have lion-like hearts, loving Christ first, His truth next, and Christ and His truth beyond all the world." —Charles Spurgeon

"A man who loves you the most is the man who tells you the most truth about yourself." —Robert Murray M'Cheyne

REPRESENTING OUR TRUE COUNTRY

Thirsty people need us to reach out and extend to them as cold water Christ's offer of citizenship in another world, a coming eternal home.

There is widespread concern about many nations' economies. And blame. But the problem is the human heart. What affects economies is the cumulative attributes of individuals that make up a nation—honesty, hard work, gratitude and care for others, rather than obsession with what we imagine we deserve. We can't solve all our nation's problems, but we can address the issues of our own hearts.

No matter what direction our earthly country may be going, it is our never-ending heavenly country that we should represent. "Instead, they were longing for a better country—a heavenly one. Therefore God is not ashamed to be called their God, for he has prepared a city for them" (Hebrews 11:16, NIV).

Peace, safety, and economic prosperity are threatened in the world's current crises. People living in the wreckage of this sin-stained Earth must realize that the world's main problem is that it's inhabited by people like us, sinners in need of redemption. They need us to reach out our hands and extend to them, as cold water to the thirsty, Christ's offer of citizenship in another world, a coming eternal home.

PERSPECTIVES FROM GOD'S WORD

"If my people who are called by my name humble themselves, and pray and seek my face and turn from their wicked ways, then I will hear from heaven and will forgive their sin and heal their land" (2 Chronicles 7:14).

"For in this tent we groan, longing to put on our heavenly dwelling…while we are at home in the body we are away from the Lord…we would rather be away from the body and at home with the Lord" (2 Corinthians 5:2, 6, 8).

PERSPECTIVES FROM GOD'S PEOPLE

"Our deepest instinct is heaven. Heaven is the ache in our bones, the splinter in our heart." —Mark Buchanan

"I must keep alive in myself the desire for my true country, which I shall not find till after death; I must never let it get snowed under or turned aside; I must make it the main object of life to press on to that other country and to help others to do the same." —C. S. Lewis

THE COURAGE TO FOLLOW HIM

Follow the Lord wherever He is leading you, then depend upon Him to give you more courage to take the next step.

It's not always pleasant to talk about the things God's Word says. When I meditate on Scripture, it's very common for me to become uncomfortable by what I am reading. But to follow Christ is not about being comfortable—it's about being sold-out to the God with the nailed-scarred hands, being radical for Him, standing up for Him, and speaking the truth in love, with grace.

Follow the Lord wherever He is leading you, then depend upon Him to give you more courage to take the next step. "If anyone serves me, he must follow me; and where I am, there will my servant be also. If anyone serves me, the Father will honor him" (John 12:26).

Whatever we lose today in humble service to Christ, we will regain a trillion times over in the long tomorrow. "If anyone would come after me, let him deny himself and take up his cross daily and follow me. For whoever would save his life will lose it, but whoever loses his life for my sake will save it" (Luke 9:23–24).

PERSPECTIVES FROM GOD'S WORD

"Whoever loses his life for my sake and the gospel's will save it" (Mark 8:35).

"Be strong in the Lord and in the strength of his might" (Ephesians 6:10).

PERSPECTIVES FROM GOD'S PEOPLE

"Courage seems a contradiction: a strong desire to live taking the form of a readiness to die." —G. K. Chesterton

"It is easier to find a score of men wise enough to discover the truth than to find one intrepid enough, in the face of opposition, to stand up for it." —A. A. Hodge

Day 57

THE ULTIMATE
RESTORATION

God is the ultimate salvage artist. He loves to restore things—and make them even better.

Because the earth is the realm where God's glory has been the most challenged and resisted, it is also the stage on which His glory will be the most graphically demonstrated. By reclaiming, restoring, and resurrecting Earth—and empowering a regenerated mankind to reign over it—God will accomplish his purpose of bringing glory to Himself. And "Of the increase of his government and of peace there will be no end" (Isaiah 9:7).

A great year-round song is "Joy to the World," because it looks forward to Christ's return and the New Earth. "No more let sins and sorrows grow… he comes to make his blessings flow far as the curse is found." Christ's redemptive work will reverse the Curse and restore the earth (2 Peter 3:13).

If God had wanted to consign Adam and Eve to Hell and start over, He could have. Instead, He chose to redeem what

He started with—the heavens, earth and mankind—to bring them back to His original purpose. God is the ultimate salvage artist. He loves to restore things—and make them even better. His perfect plan is "to unite all things in him, things in heaven and things on earth" (Ephesians 1:10).

PERSPECTIVES FROM GOD'S WORD

"…the Christ appointed for you, Jesus, whom heaven must receive until the time for restoring all the things about which God spoke by the mouth of his holy prophets long ago" (Acts 3:20–21).

"In the new world, when the Son of Man will sit on his glorious throne, you who have followed me will also sit on twelve thrones, judging the twelve tribes of Israel" (Matthew 19:28).

PERSPECTIVES FROM GOD'S PEOPLE

"The kingdom of God…does not mean merely the salvation of certain individuals nor even the salvation of a chosen group of people. It means nothing less than the complete renewal of the entire cosmos, culminating in the new heaven and the new earth." —Anthony Hoekema

"Our Lord has written the promise of the resurrection not in books alone, but in every leaf in spring-time." —Martin Luther

Day 58

STRIVING TO BE A
FAITHFUL STEWARD

Stewardship is about time, abilities, relationships, work; not just money. It is the whole Christian life.

A steward's primary goal is to be "found faithful" by his master. He proves himself faithful by wisely using the master's resources to accomplish the tasks delegated to him. Those resources include not only money but time, gifting, relationships, employment. From this perspective, stewardship isn't a narrow subcategory of the Christian life. On the contrary, stewardship is the Christian life.

God says, "it is required of stewards that they be found faithful," not successful (1 Corinthians 4:2). We must leave the results to Him. Jesus said, "For where your treasure is, there will your heart be also" (Luke 12:34). The more we invest in the things that matter to God, the more our hearts are drawn to Him. The person who puts his treasures into God's hands demonstrates love for God and others. Since his heart will follow his treasures, it's not just the lives of the needy changed by his giving—it's his own.

God pays a great deal of attention to the "little things." He numbers the hairs on our heads, cares for the lilies of the field, and is concerned with the fall of a single sparrow. As a business owner pays attention to how an employee handles the little things, God pays attention to us. What we do with a little time, a little talent, and a little money tells God a lot.

PERSPECTIVES FROM GOD'S WORD

"If then you have not been faithful in the unrighteous wealth, who will entrust to you the true riches?" (Luke 16:11).

"And he said to him, 'Well done, good servant! Because you have been faithful in a very little, you shall have authority over ten cities'" (Luke 19:17).

PERSPECTIVES FROM GOD'S PEOPLE

"The world asks, 'What does a man own?' Christ asks, 'How does he use it?'" —Andrew Murray

"All that we have is a loan from God. We are God's stewards. We are God's debtors. Let this thought sink deeply into our hearts." —J. C. Ryle

FINDING TRUE CONTENTMENT

The way to contentment in each season of life is to choose to see the advantages of our present calling in life.

Each phase of life is different, with its own challenges but also its own rewards. The way to contentment is to compare the advantages of our present calling to the disadvantages of past and future.

Sinclair Ferguson writes, "Christian contentment is the direct fruit of having no higher ambition than to belong to the Lord and to be totally at His disposal in the place He appoints, at the time He chooses, with the provision He is pleased to make."

We won't be fully content until we're home with our Beloved. But the closest we can get to contentment—and to Heaven—while we're still here as aliens and strangers on this earth, is when we come away with Jesus and get away from His substitutes. We need to tear down the idols, and give God sole occupation of the throne of our lives. "Little children, keep yourselves from idols" (1 John 5:21). True contentment comes when we're looking to only one God, the genuine article.

PERSPECTIVES FROM GOD'S WORD

"Godliness with contentment is great gain" (1 Timothy 6:6).

"For the sake of Christ, then, I am content with weaknesses, insults, hardships, persecutions, and calamities. For when I am weak, then I am strong" (2 Corinthians 12:10).

PERSPECTIVES FROM GOD'S PEOPLE

"Contentment is one of the flowers of heaven, and, if we would have it, it must be cultivated." —Charles Spurgeon

"If the sun of God's countenance shine upon me, I may well be content to be wet with the rain of affliction."
—Joseph Hall

Day 60

PURSUING THE
RIGHT PERSPECTIVE

We can and should live now with the perspective that will be ours one minute after we die.

Jesus calls His followers citizens of Heaven. When we think more about dinner out tomorrow than the banquet on the New Earth with Abraham, Isaac, and Jacob, we lose sight of Heaven and surrender the present joy that comes in anticipating it. We must fix our eyes on things that, for the present, remain invisible.

Immediately on leaving this world all who know Christ will gain the right perspective. The good news is we don't have to wait until then. We can and should live now with the perspective that will be ours one minute after we die.

Paul's admonition in Colossians 3:1 is, "Diligently, actively, single-mindedly pursue the things above"—in other words, Jesus and Heaven. Don't just have a conversation, read a book, or listen to a sermon and feel as if you've fulfilled the command. If you're going to spend the next lifetime living in Heaven, why not spend this lifetime seeking Heaven so you can eagerly anticipate and prepare for it?

PERSPECTIVES FROM GOD'S WORD

"Set your minds on things that are above, not on things that are on earth" (Colossians 3:2).

"Since you are waiting for these [the New Heavens and New Earth], be diligent to be found by him without spot or blemish, and at peace" (2 Peter 3:14).

PERSPECTIVES FROM GOD'S PEOPLE

"It becomes us to spend this life only as a journey toward heaven.... Why should we labor for or set our hearts on anything else, but that which is our proper end and true happiness?" —Jonathan Edwards

"The consideration of heaven is no mere spiritual luxury, no mere intellectual dissipation, no imaginative revelry, but is really and definitely practical and suitable...and has a real bearing on our daily life." —W. H. Griffith Thomas

About the
Author

Randy Alcorn is an author and the director of Eternal Perspective Ministries (EPM), a nonprofit ministry dedicated to teaching principles of God's Word and assisting the church in ministering to the unreached, unfed, unborn, untrained, unreconciled, and unsupported people around the world. His ministry focus is communicating the strategic importance of using our earthly time, money, possessions, and opportunities to invest in need-meeting ministries that count for eternity. He accomplishes this by analyzing, teaching, and applying biblical truth.

Before starting EPM in 1990, Randy served as a pastor for fourteen years. He holds degrees in theology and biblical studies and has taught on the adjunct faculties of Multnomah University and Western Seminary in Portland, Oregon.

Randy is the bestselling author of over forty books (seven million in print), including the novels *Deadline, Dominion*, and *Deception*, as well as *The Chasm, Safely Home*, and *Courageous*. His nonfiction works include *Heaven*; *If God is Good*; *Managing God's Money*; *Money, Possessions, and Eter-*

nity; *The Treasure Principle*; *The Grace and Truth Paradox*; and *The Law of Rewards*. Randy has written for many magazines and produces the popular magazine *Eternal Perspectives*. He's been a guest on numerous radio and television programs, including *Focus on the Family, The Bible Answer Man, Family Life Today*, and *Revive Our Hearts*.

The father of two married daughters, Karina and Angela, Randy lives in Gresham, Oregon, with his wife and best friend, Nanci. They are the proud grandparents of five grandsons: Jake, Matt, Ty, Jack, and David. Randy enjoys hanging out with his family, biking, tennis, research, and reading.

You may contact Eternal Perspective Ministries online at www.epm.org, or at 39085 Pioneer Blvd., Suite 206, Sandy, OR 97055, 503-668-5200 or toll free 1-877-376-4567.

Connect with Randy online:

Facebook: www.facebook.com/randyalcorn
Twitter: www.twitter.com/randyalcorn
Blog: www.epm.org/blog

 To view a full list of Randy's books, scan the code or visit **www.epm.org/books**.

About Eternal Perspective Ministries

Eternal Perspective Ministries (EPM) is a Bible-believing, Christ-centered nonprofit organization with two goals:

- To teach the principles of God's Word, emphasizing an eternal viewpoint;

- To reach the needy in Christ's name, calling attention to the needs of the unreached, unfed, unsupported, unborn, unreconciled, and untrained.

Royalties from Randy Alcorn's books go directly to the ministry and 100% are given away for ministry purposes: 90% to other worthy Christian organizations and 10% to EPM to help offset the costs related to the writing/researching/editing of the books, as well as to help facilitate the giving away of our books to people all over the world.

We love the fact that God uses Randy's books to change people's lives in two ways: through the reading of his words and through the giving away of his royalties. Since its inception in 1990, EPM has contributed over $6 million in book royalties to ministries around the world.

You can order all of Randy's books and products

through EPM's online store at www.epm.org. (The EPM web site also has many free resources, including articles, audio, video, pastors' kits, and more.) When you purchase Randy's books from EPM, the profits go directly to support the work of the ministry and fund our operating expenses.

Several times a year, EPM produces *Eternal Perspectives*, a 16-page color magazine filled with thought-provoking and informative articles, most authored by Randy, on a variety of subjects related to Christian living, Heaven, giving, missions, and much more. EPM also sends weekly email newsletters with the latest about Randy's books, projects, and speaking events, as well as featured family news and special promotions from EPM. You can subscribe at www.epm.org/subscribe.

You can contact Eternal Perspective Ministries online at www.epm.org, or at 39085 Pioneer Blvd., Suite 206, Sandy, OR 97055, 503-668-5200 or toll free 1-877-376-4567.

Connect with Eternal Perspective Ministries:

Facebook: www.facebook.com/EPMinistries
Twitter: www.twitter.com/epmorg
Pinterest: www.pinterest.com/randyalcorn

NONFICTION BOOKS BY RANDY ALCORN

50 Days of Heaven

Randy Alcorn brings eternity to light in 50 inspiring and thought provoking mediations that will forever change the way you think about the spectacular new universe that awaits us.

www.epm.org/50days

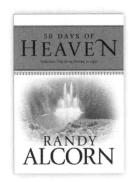

Heaven

In the most comprehensive and definitive book on Heaven to date, Randy invites you to picture Heaven the way Scripture describes it. If you've always thought of Heaven as a realm of disembodied spirits, you're in for a wonderful surprise.

www.epm.org/heavenbook

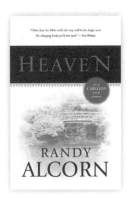

NONFICTION BOOKS
BY RANDY ALCORN

hand in Hand

A careful guide through Scripture, *hand in Hand* shows us why God's sovereignty and meaningful human choice work together in a beautiful way.

www.epm.org/handinHand

If God Is Good

Every one of us is experiencing—or will experience—suffering. In difficult times, suffering and evil beg questions about God—Why would an all-good, all-powerful God create a world full of evil and suffering?

www.epm.org/igig

NONFICTION BOOKS
BY RANDY ALCORN

Managing God's Money

Randy breaks down what the Bible
has to say about how we are to
handle our money and possessions
in a simple and easy-to-follow
format.

www.epm.org/mgm

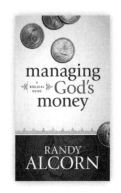

The Treasure Principle

This book introduces readers to a
revolution in material freedom and
radical generosity that will change
lives around the world. Once
readers discover the liberating joy of
giving, life will never look the same!

www.epm.org/treasure

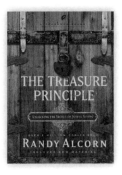

NONFICTION BOOKS
BY RANDY ALCORN

The Grace and Truth Paradox

John 1:14 boils down for us what
it means to be Christlike. It means
to be full of only two things:
Grace and Truth. It's a two-point
checklist of Christlikeness.

www.epm.org/gandt

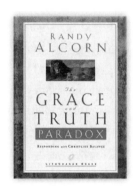

The Purity Principle

Randy Alcorn shows us why, in this
culture of impurity, the stakes are
so high—and what we can do to
experience the freedom of purity.
Includes practical guidelines as well
as advice for developing biblical
accountability.

www.epm.org/purity

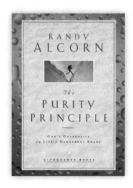

FICTION BOOKS BY RANDY ALCORN

The Chasm

The Chasm is a short-story allegory about a man on a journey to reach a special place. Illustrated by artist Mike Biegel with a dozen compelling line drawings.

www.epm.org/chasm

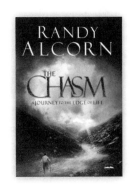

Courageous

By Randy Alcorn, Alex Kendrick, and Stephen Kendrick. Law enforcement officers Adam Mitchell, Nathan Hayes, and their partners face a challenge that none of them are truly prepared to tackle: fatherhood.

www.epm.org/courageous

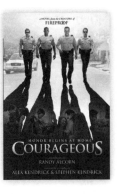

Fiction Books by Randy Alcorn

Eternity

In a dramatic rendition of the Rich Man and Lazarus story, author Randy Alcorn and artist Javier Saltares take readers into the world of first century Jerusalem and then two eternal realms. Graphic novel.

www.epm.org/eternity

Safely Home

American Ben Fielding has no idea what his brilliant old college roommate is facing in China. Thrown together in an hour of encroaching darkness, both must make choices that will determine the destinies of two men, two families, two nations, and two worlds.

www.epm.org/safelyhomebook

ALSO PUBLISHED BY ETERNAL PERSPECTIVE MINISTRIES

Does the Birth Control Pill Cause Abortions?

The question of whether the Pill causes abortions has direct bearing on untold millions of Christians, many of them prolife, who use and recommend it.

www.epm.org/bcp

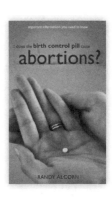

Help for Women Under Stress

By Randy and Nanci Alcorn. In this thoroughly revised and updated edition of their book originally published in 1987, Randy and Nanci give plenty of useful tips and strategies for bringing peace to the chaos of your daily life.

www.epm.org/hfwus